The Gen X Series

CYBER OLYMPIAD 4

Useful for Cyber Olympiads Conducted at School, National & International Levels

Authors
Shraddha Singh
Bunny Mehra
Peer Reviewer
Manasvi Vohra

Strictly According to the Latest Syllabus of Cyber Olympiad

V&S PUBLISHERS

Published by:

F-2/16, Ansari road, Daryaganj, New Delhi-110002
☎ 23240026, 23240027 • *Fax:* 011-23240028
info@vspublishers.com • www.vspublishers.com

Online Brandstore: amazon.in/vspublishers

Regional Office : Hyderabad
5-1-707/1, Brij Bhawan (Beside Central Bank of India Lane)
Bank Street, Koti, Hyderabad - 500 095
☎ 040-24737290
vspublishershyd@gmail.com

Follow us on:   

BUY OUR BOOKS FROM: AMAZON FLIPKART

ISBN 978-93-579406-2-7
New Edition

DISCLAIMER

While every attempt has been made to provide accurate and timely information in this book, neither the author nor the publisher assumes any responsibility for errors, unintended omissions or commissions detected therein. The author and publisher makes no representation or warranty with respect to the comprehensiveness or completeness of the contents provided.

All matters included have been simplified under professional guidance for general information only, without any warranty for applicability on an individual. Any mention of an organization or a website in the book, by way of citation or as a source of additional information, doesn't imply the endorsement of the content either by the author or the publisher. It is possible that websites cited may have changed or removed between the time of editing and publishing the book.

Results from using the expert opinion in this book will be totally dependent on individual circumstances and factors beyond the control of the author and the publisher.

It makes sense to elicit advice from well informed sources before implementing the ideas given in the book. The reader assumes full responsibility for the consequences arising out from reading this book.

For proper guidance, it is advisable to read the book under the watchful eyes of parents/guardian. The buyer of this book assumes all responsibility for the use of given materials and information.

Printed at : Param Offsetters, Okhla, New Delhi–110020

Publisher's Note

The current decade has firmly established V&S Publishers as one of the Leading Publishers of General Trade Mass Appeal Books across popular genres along with Academic Books for school children. Having been in publishing trade for over 40 years we understand the need of the hour when it comes to Books. After successfully publishing over 600 titles in a rather short time span of 5 years and establishing a pan India network of booksellers & distributors including ecommerce platforms viz – Amazon, Flipkart etc; an extensive market research lead us to publishing our Bestselling Series ever – OLYMPIAD BOOKS.

The Olympiad Series launched 4 years back under our GEN X SERIES Imprint gained widespread popularity amongst students and teachers immediately owing to its rich, high quality content and unique presentation. Published for Classes 1-10 across subjects English, Maths, Science & Computers, these books are holistic in nature and unlike run of the mill workbooks in the market, which are mere replicas of one another, these books deal with the content in a much comprehensive manner. Recourse to the 'Principles of Applied Psychology of Student Learning' has been utilised to upgrade levels of conceptual understanding in all designated subjects among class 1 to 10 students.

Encouraged by this huge acceptability of our Olympiad Series among parents and students and after revolutionising the way Olympiad books were written and published, we at V&S Publishers decided to take this to the next level.

We present to you Brand New Edition of our book – **CYBER OLYMPIAD CLASS 4.**

Each book originally written by Subject Matter Expert, is now further Peer Reviewed by top School Teachers and HODs to eliminate the slightest of errors that were present earlier. Furthermore to ensure authenticity and accuracy of content the book is now completely revised and reformatted as per the guidelines of the examining body. The New and Revised Olympiad Book is now suited to Olympiad examinations conducted at School Level, National Level or International Level by any and all organisations/companies.

The New Edition of this Cyber Olympiad Class 4 is written in a Guide like pattern with images and illustrations at every step & is divided into different sections. Each chapter comes with Basic Theory and Solved Examples. Multiple Choice Questions with their Answer Keys and Solutions are liberally included. In order to help students become aware of and to simulate the actual exam conditions, a bunch of OMR Sheets have been enclosed with the book as well.

Amalgamation of Technology with Content has always been at the forefront for V&S Publishers and our new Student Portal for Olympiad Practice–**www.vsexamprep.com** is further testimony to that. We recommend students logging in and using it to their benefit.

P.S. While every care has been taken to ensure correctness of content, if you come across any error, howsoever minor, anywhere in the book, do not hesitate to discuss with your teachers while pointing that out to us in no uncertain terms.

We wish you All The Best!

Contents

SECTION 1: COMPUTERS AND IT

SECTION 2: LOGICAL REASONING

SECTION 3: ACHIEVERS' SECTION

SECTION 1
COMPUTERS AND IT

Fundamentals of Computer

1

Chapter Outline:

- Parts of Computer
- Software
- Hardware
- Input Devices
- Output Devices
- Memory
- Multiple Choice Questions

Computer is an electronic machine. It can receive data from its user, process it and display results. It can also store and work with large amounts of information.

Parts of Computer

A computer needs two main parts to operate or function. They are hardware and software. A computer hardware is a part of the computer that you can physically see or touch. The software is a computer program that tells computer hardware how to operate.

Software

Software is a set of data or instructions that is processed by the hardware components to perform a task. Software is a set of programs that perform some specific functions along with given input. A person who develops or creates a software is called a software programmer or a software engineer.

There are two types of software. They are the system software and the application software. You will learn about these software in detail in higher classes.

The chart given below shows you the different types of softwares.

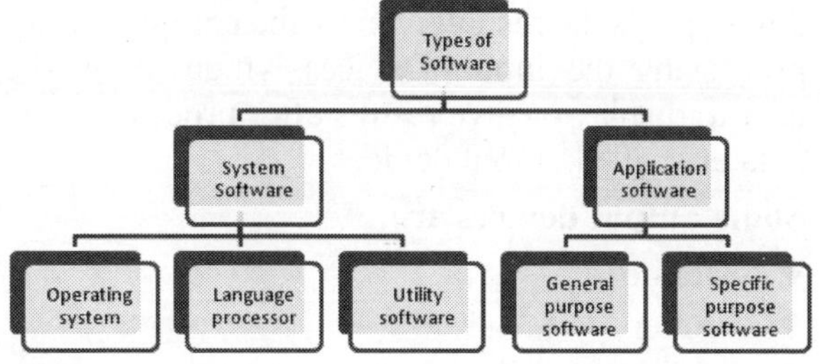

Hardware

The following are some hardware devices of a computer system:

Central Processing Unit (CPU)

The CPU is the computer's main chip or the brain that controls the functioning of all its other parts. It calculates and processes information and instructs the peripheral devices what to do. The speed at which it processes information is measured in Megahertz (MHz) and Gigahertz (GHz).

Hard Disk

The hard disk is the computer's main storage device. It is fitted inside the cabinet alongside the CPU.

The computer hardware includes all the input and the output devices and also the CPU.

Input Devices

An input is a set of data given to the computer to perform a task. Devices which allow the user to feed instruction or data into the computer are called input devices.

Some common input devices are:

- Keyboard
- Joystick
- Trackball
- Mouse
- Touch panel monitor
- Microphone
- Optical mark reader
- Light pen
- Scanner
- Card reader
- Digital camera
- Barcode reader
- Magnetic Ink Character Reader (MICR).

Output Devices

An output is the result given by the computer after processing the input. Devices which allow the user to display or give results after processing the data are called output devices.

Some output devices are:

- Monitor
- Printer
- Voice synthesizer
- Plotter
- Speakers

Let us learn about some common input devices.

Mouse

Acts as a hand-held pointing device and controls the actions of the cursor on your computer screen.

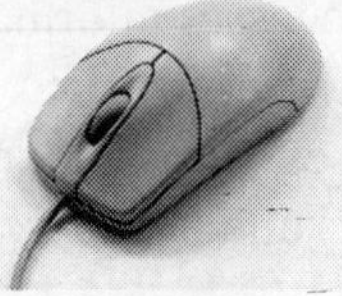

Keyboard

Lets you input your information and commands into a computer by pressing the keys on it.

Digital camera

Lets you take pictures and transfer them to a computer.

Mentioned below are some output devices.

Monitor

Looks like a TV screen. The monitor is where text and images and videos appear.

Printer

Transfers processed information to printed page.

Speakers

Allow you to hear the sounds produced by the sound card.

Plotter

Draws picture on paper based on commands from a computer.

Memory

Memory is a computer's temporary storage place, where it stores information so that the CPU can process it as and when required. There are two main types of memory on your computer. They are RAM (Random Access Memory) and ROM (Read Only Memory).

RAM (Random Access Memory) or Primary Memory

This memory is volatile, which means unsaved data disappears when you shut down the computer.

ROM (Read Only Memory) or Secondary Memory

This memory is non volatile, which means data can be retrieved even when you shut down the computer.

Multiple Choice Questions

1. Identify the given device.

(a) RAM
(b) UPS
(c) Power supply unit
(d) Heater

2. The device shown in the figure is a _____.

(a) Modem (b) Motherboard
(c) Display card (d) Sound card

3. Identify this device.

(a) Pin cushion (b) RAM
(c) CPU (d) Battery

4. Identify this device.

(a) Motherboard
(b) Fan
(c) CPU
(d) Heat Sink Processor Fan

5. Zip disks were launched with the capacity of _____.

(a) 100 MB (b) 1 GB
(c) 1 TB (d) 1 MB

6. Identify this device.

(a) RAM (b) ROM
(c) Hard disk (d) Floppy disk

7. Floppy disk drives have been superseded by which of the following data storage methods?

(a) USB flash drives
(b) External hard disk drives
(c) Optical disks
(d) All of these

Directions (8–9): Given below is an image of a computer. Answer the questions that follow.

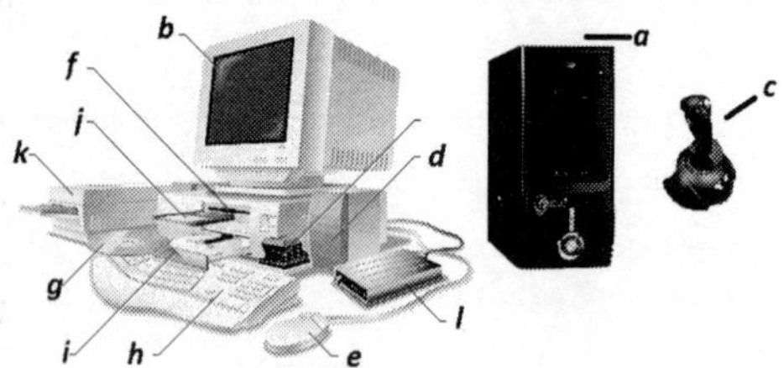

8. Which of the following input devices are connected with the computer?

(a) e (b) h
(c) j (d) All of these

9. Match the following.

Column-I	**Column –II**
(i) a	(a) Mouse
(ii) c	(b) Keyboard
(iii) h	(c) Joystick
(iv) e	(d) CPU

(a) (i)–(d), (ii)–(b), (iii)–(a), (iv)–(c)
(b) (i)–(d), (ii)–(a), (iii)–(b), (iv)–(c)
(c) (i)–(d), (ii)–(a), (iii)–(c), (iv)–(b)
(d) (i)–(d), (ii)–(c), (iii)–(b), (iv)–(a)

10. Which input device can be used to read data from book covers?

(a) Barcode reader
(b) Optical Mark Reader
(c) Scanner
(d) Keyboard

11. Which type of an input device would be most suitable in a fast food restaurant?

(a) Barcode reader
(b) Concept keyboard
(c) Keyboard
(d) Mouse

12. The most appropriate input device for collecting environmental data is _____.
    (a) Barcode reader
    (b) Mouse
    (c) Keyboard
    (d) Sensor
13. Which printer would you recommend to your school administrative department to print large quantities of black and white mail merged letters?
    (a) Inkjet
    (b) Laser
    (c) Plotter
    (d) Dot matrix
14. The device shown here is popularly known as MFD. The full form of a MFD is _____.

    (a) Multi-Function Device
    (b) Multi-Feature Device
    (c) Multi-Feature Disk
    (d) Major Function Device
15. Identify this device.

    (a) Barcode reader
    (b) Plasma monitor
    (c) Oscilloscope
    (d) Overhead projector
16. Identify this device

    (a) USB card
    (b) Memory card reader
    (c) Pen drive
    (d) Portable hard disk
17. Identify this device.

    (a) Flatbed scanner
    (b) Handheld scanner
    (c) Sensor
    (d) Web camera
18. Identify this device.

    (a) Touchscreen
    (b) Scanner
    (c) Calculator
    (d) Concept keyboard
19. Parts of a computer which you can touch and feel are called _____.
    (a) Hardware (b) Software
    (c) Firmware (d) Utility
20. A tiny piece of silicon which has electric circuits on it is called _____.
    (a) Wafer (b) Chip
    (c) Bit (d) Memory
21. Software can be defined as _____.
    (a) Programs needed to run a computer
    (b) The parts of a computer system that you can touch
    (c) The peripherals and operating system of the computer
    (d) The machines and programs making up a computer system
22. What does a computer require in order to run a peripheral properly?
    (a) An operating system
    (b) A device driver
    (c) A memory upgrade
    (d) A fast processor

23. When an application is loaded on a computer, what is it loaded into?
(a) Hard drive (b) Monitor
(c) ROM (d) RAM

24. A computer must have _____.
(a) A printer attached to it
(b) An operating system
(c) A word processing software
(d) A virus checking program

25. Which hardware will you use for bulk printing in large computer centres?
(a) Plotter
(b) Line printer
(c) Drum printer
(d) Dot Matrix printer

26. Match the following.

Column-I	Column-II
(i) Optical Mark Reader	(a) Printing out car designs
(ii) Plotter	(b) Making backup copies of data
(iii) Magnetic Strip Reader	(c) Reading information from student's exam answers
(iv) Touchscreen	(d) Reading information from credit cards
(v) Zip drive	(e) Choosing from a set of options

(a) (i)–(c), (ii)–(a), (iii)–(d), (iv)–(b), (v)–(e)
(b) (i)–(c), (ii)–(d), (iii)–(a), (iv)–(b), (v)–(e)
(c) (i)–(c), (ii)–(e), (iii)–(b), (iv)–(a), (v)–(d)
(d) (i)–(c), (ii)–(a), (iii)–(d), (iv)–(e), (v)–(b)

27. In which of the following devices is a ball on the top rolled with a finger to move the cursor on the screen?

(a) 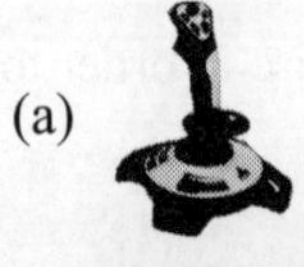 (b) 

(c)   (d) 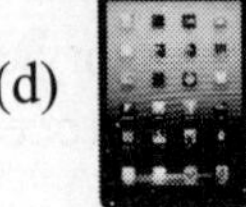

28. To take out a CD from a CD ROM drive, click the _____ command.
(a) Close (b) Open
(c) Eject (d) Pause

29. Which of the following is NOT a pointing device?

(a)  (b) 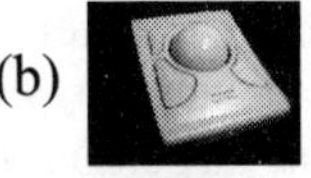

(c)  (d)

30. What does the CPU of a computer actually process?
(a) Device drivers
(b) Bits and bytes
(c) Applications
(d) ASCII

31. Which of the following is a computer hardware?
(a) Computer desk
(b) Processor
(c) Mouse pad
(d) MS-office

32. Match the following.

Column-I	Column- II
(i) 	(a) Output sound from the computer
(ii)	(b) Used to write directly on the screen
(iii) 	(c) Input and output device
(iv) 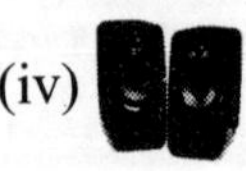	(d) Input sound/voice to the computer

(a) (i)–(c), (ii)–(d), (iii)–(b), (iv)–(a)
(b) (i)–(c), (ii)–(d), (iii)–(a), (iv)–(b)
(c) (i)–(c), (ii)–(a), (iii)–(d), (iv)–(b)
(d) (i)–(d), (ii)–(c), (iii)–(b), (iv)–(a)

33. What is a peripheral?
(a) Paper used in a printer
(b) Any device connected to a computer but not a part of it
(c) All websites available on internet
(d) All the software running on the computer

34. Which of the following storage devices is also used for backup?
   (a) Processor
   (b) RAM
   (c) ROM
   (d) Hard disk
35. Which of the following is NOT an example of a storage device?
   (a) Printer
   (b) Floppy disk
   (c) DVD
   (d) CD
36. Identify the device.
   (a) Flatbed Plotter
   (b) Drum Plotter
   (c) Thermal Plotter
   (d) Scan Plotter
37. Which type of storage device holds the least amount of information?
   (a) CD ROM
   (b) Flash drive
   (c) Hard disk
   (d) Floppy disk
38. Select the INCORRECT match.
   (a) 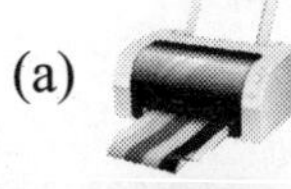 Printer vector graphics
   (b) 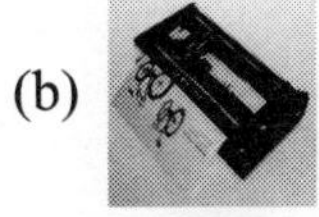 Industrial design vector
   (c) 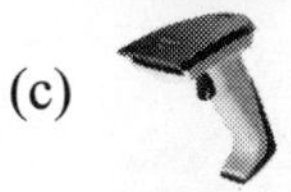 Swipe debit card
   (d)  Printing letter
39. You are playing music on your computer. However, you cannot hear the music. Which of the following devices should be checked?
   (a)  (b) 
   (c)  (d) 
40. An input device that utilizes a light sensitive detector to select objects on a display screen is
   (a)  (b) 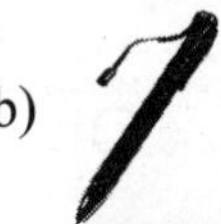
   (c) (d) 
41. What are the two types of software?
   (i) Application Software
   (ii) System Software
   (iii) Operating System Software
   (a) (i) and (ii)
   (b) (i) and (iii)
   (c) (ii) and (iii)
   (d) All of these
42. What do application programs do?
   (a) Enable the computer to talk to the hardware.
   (b) Enable the user to perform a task.
   (c) Enable software and hardware to run simultaneously.
   (d) All of these
43. When you run into problems with software, which menu option should you choose?
   (a) Options (b) Help
   (c) File (d) Print
44. What is a software?
   (a) A type of computer code
   (b) A computer language
   (c) A set of instructions for your computer
   (D) A cover for the computer
45. Which of the following is a software?
   (a)  (b) 

   (c)  (d) 
46. Windows 7 is what type of software?
   (a) Utility software
   (b) Application software
   (c) System software
   (d) Package

47. Videos and music on a computer can be played on which of the following software?

(a) Microsoft Office
(b) CorelDRAW X4
(c) 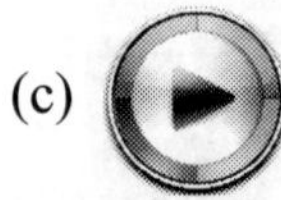
(d) Norton ANTI

48. Windows is a WYSIWYG operating system. WYSIWYG stands for _____.
(a) What you see is what you get
(b) Where you sit is where you get
(c) What you say is what you get
(d) What you show is what you get

49. The software which controls and organizes the working of a computer is called an _____.
(a) Application software
(b) Operating system
(c) DTP software
(d) Utility software

50. What type of software is an anti-virus software?
(a) Utility software
(b) Application software
(c) Operating system
(d) None of these

Evolution of Computer

2

Chapter Outline:

- ❒ Computers in Olden Days
- ❒ Generation of Computers
- ❒ Multiple Choice Questions

Computers in Olden Days

The computer was not invented to entertain us but it was invented to solve complicated calculations. It was used to keep records of calculations or perform repetitive calculations. With every development and passage of time, the computer became more advanced, user friendly and better than each previous model. Let us get an overview of key concepts which takes you through the evolution of computers.

Name	Developer/Inventor	Features
Abacus	Chinese in 16th century	First calculating device used for addition and subtraction. It has a series of thin rods each containing a number of beads. These beads are moved up and down to keep record of calculations. Its only purpose was to count and keep track of money.
Napier's bones	John Napier	For this a rod was made of bones. It had numbers written on it. It was used for multiplication and division.
Pascaline calculator	Blaise Pascal	It was also called the numerical wheel calculator. It was used for addition, subtraction, multiplication and division.
Leibnitz calculator	Gottfried Wilhelm Leibnitz	It was the first calculator to perform all four the arithmetical operations – addition, subtraction, multiplication and division.
Difference engine	Charles Babbage	It was the first automatic calculating machine. It performed complex mathematical calculations.
Analytical engine	Charles Babbage	First general computer which had same features as modern computer. Input > Process > Output > Storage

Generation of Computers

The development of computing devices is categorized into generations. Each generation showcases a major technological improvement. There are five generations of computers. They are as shown in the organizational chart given below.

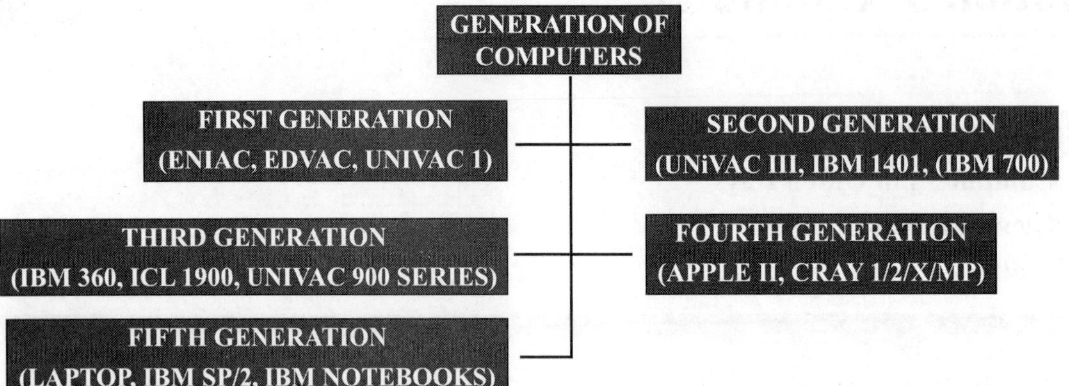

First generation computers: They were huge in size and occupied almost the entire room. They employed vacuum tubes for processing data and storage. Their operation was expensive and consumed enormous amounts of electricity. They relied on machine language for operation.

Second generation computers: They employed transistors and relied on symbolic language such as assembly language rather than machine language. They were smaller, cheaper, faster and energy efficient.

Third generation computers: They employed integrated chip. The transistors were miniaturized and placed on silicon chips which made processing faster and more efficient.

Fourth generation computers: The microprocessor marked the arrival of fourth generation computers. Many integrated chips were placed on silicon chips.

Fifth generation computers: They are supercomputers with artificial intelligence. They can recognize voices, fingerprints, etc.

Multiple Choice Questions

1. A special electronic machine that accepts instructions, processes the information and puts out the information is called ______.
   (a) System
   (b) Computer
   (c) Machine
   (d) Lock
2. Which computer amongst the following will be the fastest?
   (a) Processor speed 1 GHz, hard disk 200 GB
   (b) RAM 4 GB
   (c) Processor speed 2 GHz, RAM 2 GB
   (d) Processor speed 600 MHz
3. Speed of a processor is measured in which of the following units?
   (a) Megabytes or Gigabytes
   (b) Kilometres per hour
   (c) Bits or Bytes
   (d) Megahertz or Gigahertz
4. Which of the following is NOT an example of fourth generation computer?
   (a) IBM 4341
   (b) APPLE II
   (c) IBM360
   (d) PUP 11
5. Napier's Bones is so named because it was invented by ______.
   (a) John Napier
   (b) Blaise Pascal
   (c) Thomas Napier
   (d) Thomas Abacus
6. Which of the following determines the power of a computer?
   (a) Speed of its processor and capacity of ROM
   (b) Capacity of hard disk
   (c) Speed of its process and operating system
   (d) Speed of its processor and capacity of RAM
7. The 'Abacus' is derived from the Greek word ______.
   (a) Baxa (b) Abax
   (c) Abac (d) Abacako
8. This device which was made up of movable wheels is called ______. 
   (a) Abacus
   (b) Pascaline
   (c) Analytical engine
   (d) Difference engine
9. Identify this 19th century machine. 
   (a) Pascaline
   (b) Difference engine
   (c) Abacus
   (d) MARK-1
10. Which of the following calculating devices was invented by Sir John Napier?
    (a)  (b) 
    (c)  (d) 
11. The first mechanical calculator invented by Sir Blaise Pascal was known as ______.
    (a) Pascaline
    (b) Analytical engine
    (c) Napier's Bones
    (d) Abacus
12. Which of the following was also known as the first general purpose mechanical computer?
    (a) Abacus
    (b) Analytical engine
    (c) Scientific calculator
    (D) Mark-1

13. This was the first electronic computer that used the concept of a stored program. It was called the ______.
(a) EDVAC
(b) ENIAC
(c) EDSAC
(d) None of these

14. How is a generation of computers classified?
(a) By the devices used in memory and processor
(b) The accuracy of the computer
(c) The model of the computer
(d) By the speed of the computer

15. MARK-I was the first electro-mechanical computer. It was invented by ______.
(a) Howard H. Aiken
(b) J. Presper Eckert
(c) John Napier
(d) Charles Babbage

16. This was the first electronic general purpose computer conceived and designed by John Mauchly and J. Presper Eckert. It was called the ______.
(a) ENIAC
(b) UNIVAC
(c) EDVAC
(d) EDSAC

17. Which of the following PCs has a touchpad as an input device?

(a) (b)

(c) (d)

18. What is the full form of ENIAC?
(a) Electronic Neutronic Inventronic Analytical Computer
(b) Electronic Number Integrating Analysis Computer
(c) Electron Number Inventory and Computing
(d) Electronic Numerical Integrator and Computer

19. This image displays the CRAY 1. CRAY 1 is a ______.

(a) Mainframe computer
(b) Supercomputer
(c) Tablet computer
(d) Mini computer

20. ______ and ______ are supercomputers made in India.
(a) PARAM, VIKRAM
(b) PARAM, ANURAG
(c) PARAM, DHARAM
(d) KALAM, BHABHA

21. This is a computer which is lighter than a laptop. It can easily fit into bags, briefcases and pockets. This is called a ______.

(a) Supercomputer
(b) Desktop computer
(c) Surface computer
(d) Palmtop computer

22. What is this device called?

(a) Microchip
(b) Vacuum tube
(c) Transistor
(d) VLSI

23. UNIVAC stands for ______.
(a) Universe of Automatic Computers
(b) Universal Automatic Computer
(c) Universal Variable Computer
(d) Unitary Variation Computer

24. The transistor was invented by ______.
    (a) John Bardeen
    (b) Walter Houser Brattain
    (c) William Shockley
    (d) All of these

25. The second generation computers depended on ______.
    (a) Vacuum tubes
    (b) Transistors
    (c) Microprocessors
    (d) Integrated circuits

MS Word 2010

3

Chapter Outline:

❒ MS Word Window
❒ Ribbon
❒ Multiple Choice Questions

MS Word Window

Microsoft Word is a word processor developed by Microsoft. It was first released in 1983 under the name Multi-Tool Word. It lets you create, edit and share work quickly with others. It can also help you do the following.

- Check spelling and grammar
- Insert tables
- Insert images or pictures and different shapes
- Print in different formats

Following is the basic window which appears when you start MS Word. Components of the window are labelled with their names.

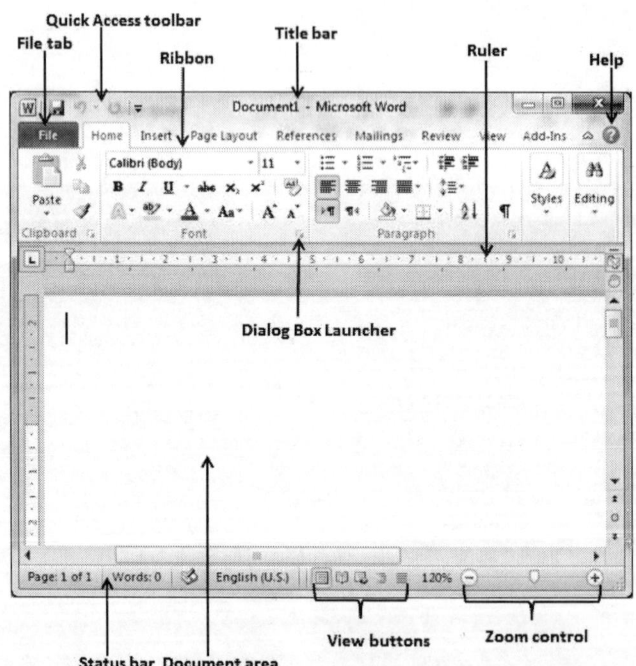

File Tab

The File tab replaces the Office button from Word 2007. You can click it to check **Backstage view**, which helps you open or save files, create new documents, print a document and perform other file-related operations.

Quick Access Toolbar

This you will find just above the **File tab** and its purpose is to provide access to Word's most frequently used commands.

Ribbon

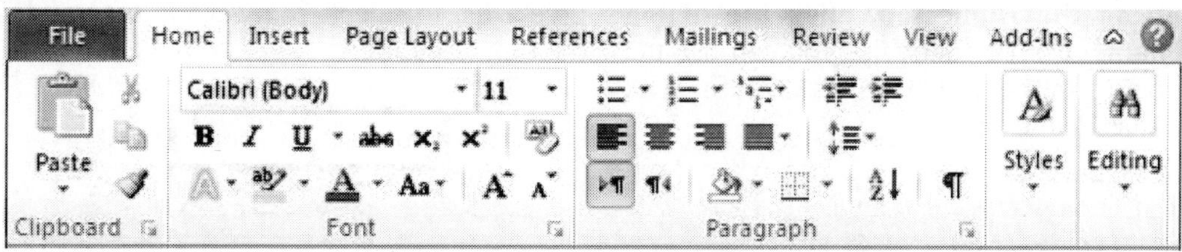

Ribbon contains commands organized in three components

- **Tabs:** They appear across the top of the Ribbon and contain groups of related commands. Home, Insert, Page Layout are example of ribbon tabs.
- **Groups:** They organize related commands; each group name appears below the group on the Ribbon. For example, group of commands related to fonts.
- **Commands:** Commands appear within each group as mentioned above.

Title bar

This lies at the top of the window. Title bar shows the program and document titles.

Rulers

Word has two rulers – a **horizontal ruler** and a **vertical ruler**. The horizontal ruler appears just beneath the Ribbon and is used to set margins and tab stops. The vertical ruler appears on the left edge of the Word window and is used to set the vertical position of elements on the page.

Help

The **Help Icon** can be used to get Word-related help anytime you need.

Zoom Control

Zoom control lets you zoom in for a closer look at your text. The zoom control consists of a slider that you can slide left or right to zoom in or out, – and + buttons you can click to increase or decrease the zoom factor.

View buttons

The group of five buttons located to the left of the Zoom control, near the bottom of the screen, lets you switch among Word's various document viewing modes.

Document area

This is the area where you type. The flashing vertical bar is called the **insertion point** and it represents the position where text will appear when you type.

Status bar

This displays document information as well as the insertion point position. From left to right, this bar contains the total number of pages and words in the document, language, etc.

Dialog box launcher

This appears as a very small arrow in the lower-right corner of many groups on the Ribbon. Clicking this button opens a dialog box or task pane that provides more options about the group.

Formatting a Word document

In Word 2010, to format a document there are different ways:

- **In your document, select the text you want to format -** You can select text in a number of ways. For example, click-and-drag over the text you want to select.

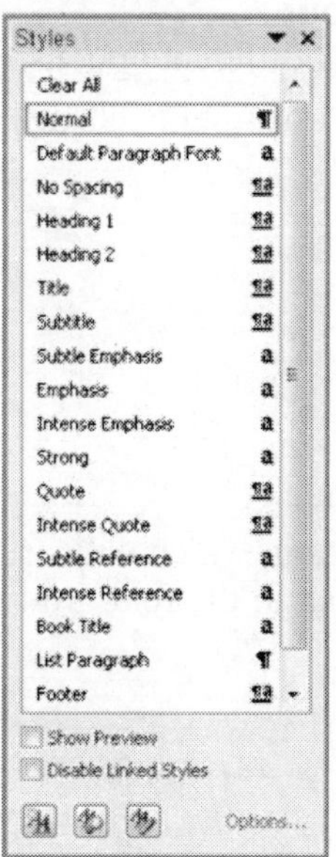

- **In the lower-right corner of the Styles group on the Home tab, click the dialog box launcher.** Alternatively, you can use the keyboard shortcut Ctrl+Shift+Alt+S. The Styles task pane opens.

- **Click the Options link in the lower right corner of the Styles task pane.** The Styles Pane Options dialog box opens.
- **Select the option All Styles from the Select Styles to Show drop-down list.** Or, if you want to keep the list shorter, choose the option In Use or In Current Document.
- **Click OK.** If you chose the All Styles option, the Styles task pane is updated to list every dang doodle style available in Word. It has quite a few of them.
- **Select a style from the Styles task pane.** After you choose a style, your document's text is reformatted to reflect that style. That style is applied to the selected text.
- **To dismiss the Styles task pane, click the X (Close) button in its upper-right corner.** The Styles task pane disappears.

The Font Group

Let us check out different options of Font group.

Change Case: It is used to change the case of the selected word.

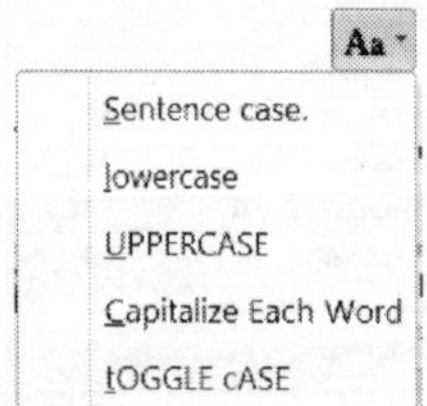

Clear Formatting, which will strip the effects of the other buttons in the font group from selected text.

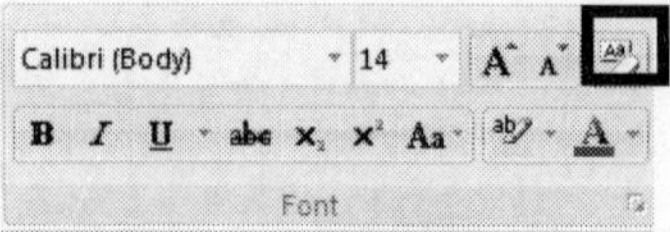

Font Type and Size: You can click on them to give a list to select from for the type and size of the font to be used.

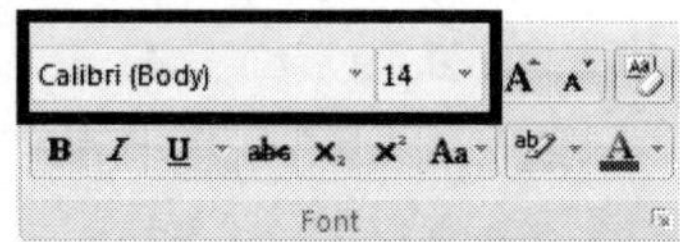

Increase/Decrease size: These two buttons will increase/decrease the size of selected text.

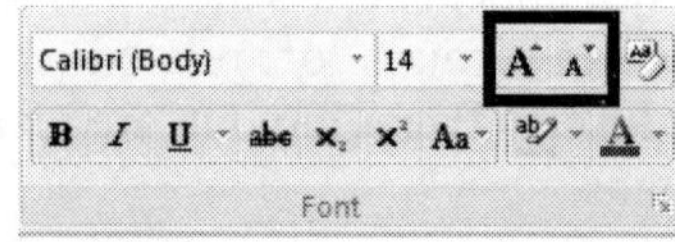

Bold/Italic: These two buttons apply **Bold** or *Italic* formatting to text.

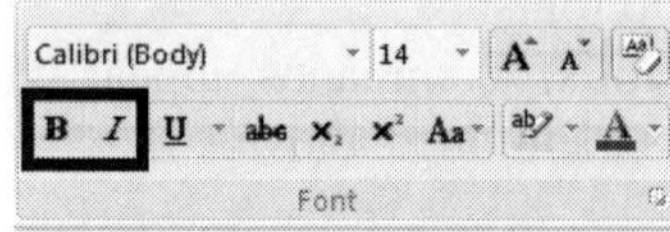

Underline: It is used to underline the selected text.

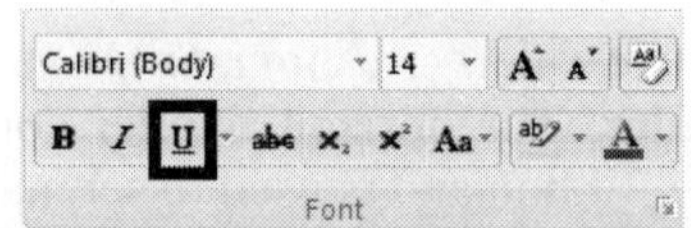

Font Color: Using **Font Color**, color of the font can be changed.

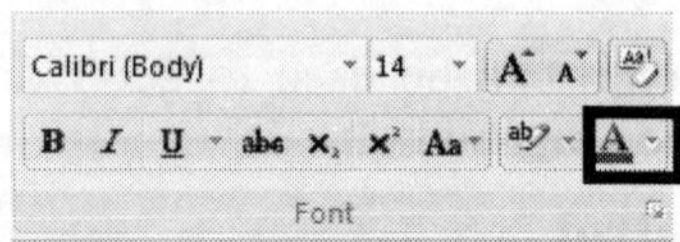

Format Painter

Format Painter is a tool used when you want to copy formatting from one item to another.

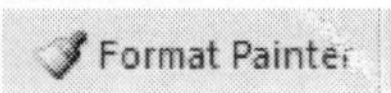

Finding and replacing text

When you're working with longer documents, it can be difficult and time consuming to locate a specific word or phrase. Word can automatically search your document using the **Find** feature, and it even allows you to change words or phrases using **Replace**.

To find text:

1. From the **Home** tab, click the **Find** command. The **navigation** pane will appear on the left side of the screen.

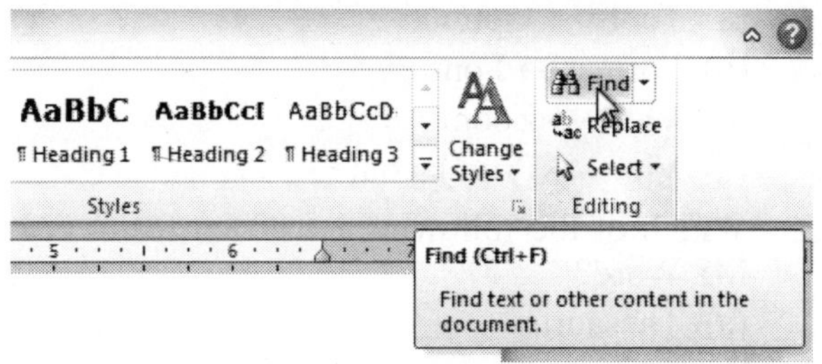

2. Type the text you want to find in the field at the top of the navigation pane.
3. If the text is found in the document, it will be highlighted in yellow, and a preview will appear in the navigation pane.
4. If the text appears more than once, you can click the **arrows** on the navigation pane to step through the results.

To replace text:

1. From the **Home** tab, click the **Replace** command. The **Find and Replace** dialog box will appear.

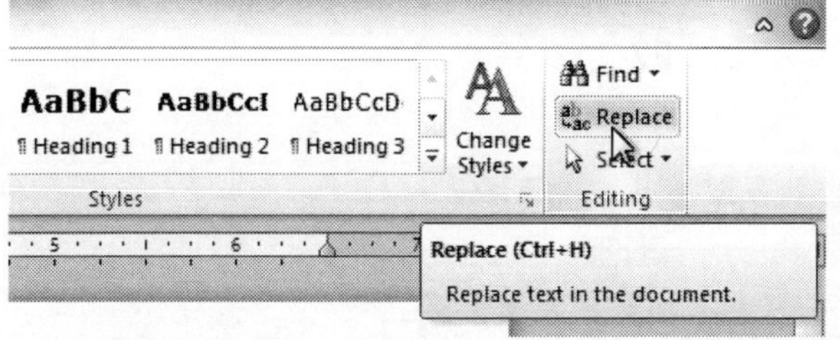

2. Type the text you want to find in the **Find what** field.
3. Type the text you want to replace it with in the **Replace with** field.
4. Click **Find Next** and then **Replace** to replace text. You can also click **Replace All** to replace all instances within the document.

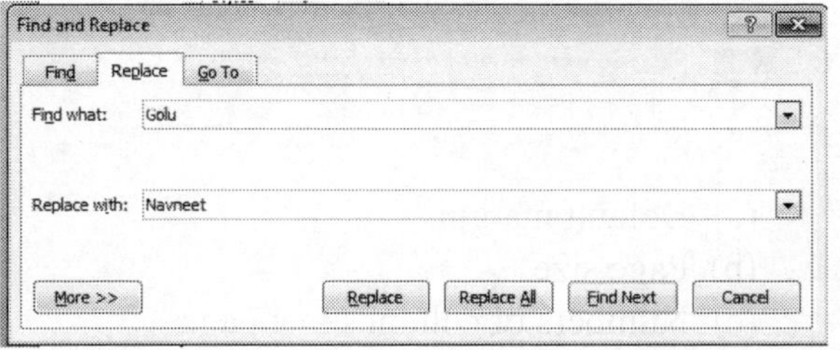

Checking Spelling and Grammar

To start a check of the spelling and grammar in your file just press F7 or follow these steps:

1. Open MS Word Program, click the **Review** tab on the ribbon.
2. Click **Spelling** or **Spelling & Grammar**.

3. If the program finds spelling mistakes, a dialog box appears with the first misspelled word found by the spelling checker.
4. After you decide how to resolve the misspelling (ignoring it, adding it to the program's dictionary, or changing it), the program moves to the next misspelled word.

Using Thesaurus

The thesaurus tool in Word 2010 allows you to select a word in your document, then look that word up in the thesaurus. You can then choose from a number of potential synonyms offered by Word and insert them in place of the selected word in your document.

- Open your document in Word 2010.
- Select the word for which you wish to find a synonym.
- Click the **Review** tab at the top of the window.
- Click the **Thesaurus** button in the **Proofing** section of the Office ribbon.

- Hover your mouse over the word that you wish to use from the column at the right side of the screen, click the arrow next to it and click the **Insert** option.

Multiple Choice Questions

1. Given below is the title bar of an MS Word document. It displays the ______ of the active document.

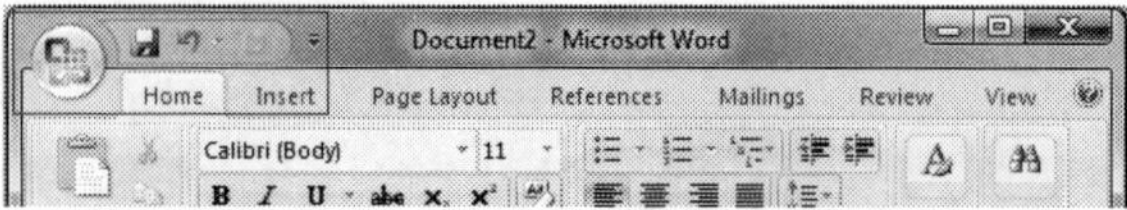

(a) Area (b) Color
(c) Height (d) Name

Directions (2-4): View the following picture and answer the questions that follow.

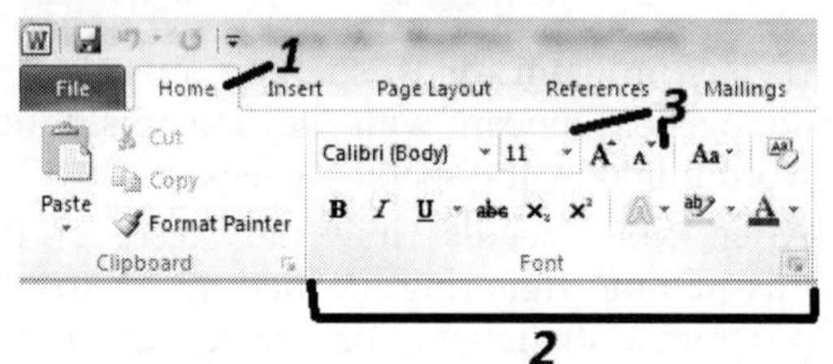

2. The menu system containing tabs and commands is called the ______.
   (a) Menu Bar
   (b) Ribbon
   (c) Command Prompt
   (d) System Bar
3. In the image shown above, Clipboard, Font, Paragraph are names of ______.
   (a) Tabs (b) Commands
   (c) Groups (d) Ribbon
4. Match the components of the ribbon listed in Column-II with the corresponding labels in Column-I.

Column-I	**Column-II**
(i) 1	(a) Command
(ii) 2	(b) Tabs
(iii) 3	(c) Groups

   (a) (i) – (a), (ii) – (c), (iii) – (b)
   (b) (i) – (b), (ii) – (a), (iii) – (c)
   (c) (i) – (b), (ii) – (c), (iii) – (a)
   (d) (i) – (c), (ii) – (b), (iii) – (a)
5. The text styles are displayed in the ______ group of the Home tab.
   (a) Paragraph (b) Font
   (c) Editing (d) Styles
6. To view several pages of your document side by side, you should use ______.
   (a) Tools → Options
   (b) Format → Font
   (c) View → Zoom
   (d) View → Print layout
7. Which of the following is NOT a feature of MS Word?
   (a) Thesaurus
   (b) Britannica
   (c) Symbols
   (d) Bullets and Numbering
8. The Thesaurus provides a list of ______ for a given word.
   (a) Antonyms
   (b) Synonyms
   (c) Verbs
   (d) Both (a) & (b)
9. What is the shortcut key to open Thesaurus?

   (a) 

   (b) 

   (c) 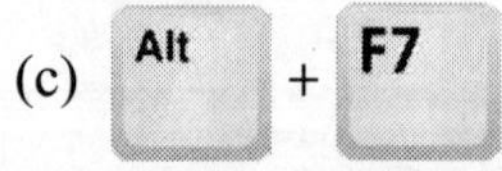

   (d) 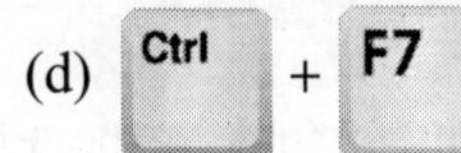

10. Which of the following options is not found in the File tab?
    (a) Print (b) Close
    (c) Edit (d) New
11. The Page Setup group is used to change the ______.

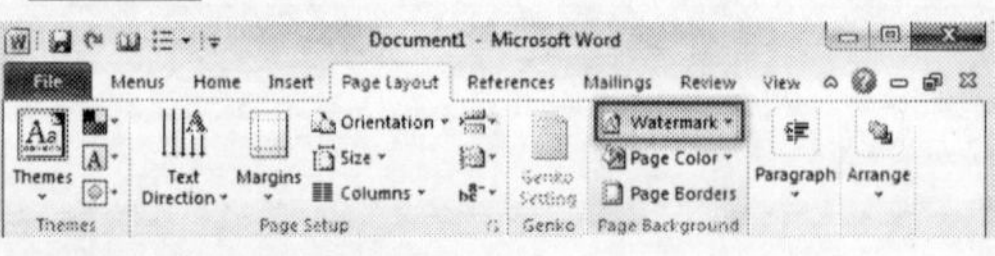

    (a) Default margins
    (b) Page size
    (c) Numbers of columns in a page
    (d) All of these

12. What is the shortcut key to replace a word or text in the document?

(a) 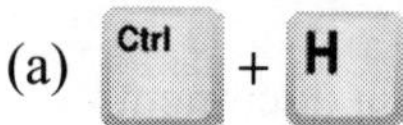

(b) Ctrl + F

(c) Ctrl + K

(d) Ctrl + A

13. Under which group of the Home tab do you find the 'Find' button?
(a) Font
(b) Paragraph
(c) Clipboard
(d) Editing

14. What is the numbering 1, 2, …., 7 shown in this image?

1. GOLU GOLU GOLU GOLU
2. GOLU GOLU GOLU GOLU GOLU GOLU GOLU GOLU GOLU GOLU
3. GOLU GOLU GOLU GOLU GOLU GOLU GOLU GOLU GOLU GOLU
4. GOLU GOLU GOLU GOLU GOLU GOLU GOLU GOLU GOLU GOLU GO GOLU
5. GOLU GOLU GOLU GOLU GOLU GOLU GOLU GOLU GOLU GOLU GO GOLU
6. GOLU GOLU GOLU GOLU GOLU GOLU GOLU GOLU GOLU GOLU GO GOLU
7. GOLU GOLU GOLU GOLU GOLU GOLU GOLU GOLU GOLU GOLU GO GOLU

(a) They are sentence numbers for each sentence in the file.
(b) They are line numbers shown for each line of the text.
(c) It is numbered text inserted by the author of the above text.
(d) All of these

15. To insert a symbol like ©, which tab should you use?
(a) Home
(b) Insert
(c) Design
(d) Page layout

16. The Header and Footer group is found in which tab of the ribbon?
(a) Home
(b) Layout
(c) Design
(d) Insert

17. How can you format a table?
(a) Change the row height
(b) Change the column width
(c) Apply border and shading
(d) All of these

18. In MS Word Table, which key is used to move to the next cell?
(a) Tab (b) Function
(c) Space (d) Enter

19. A horizontal series of cells in a table is called ______.
(a) Horizontal (b) Column
(c) Row (d) Cell

20. What is the name of the icon shown by the arrow?

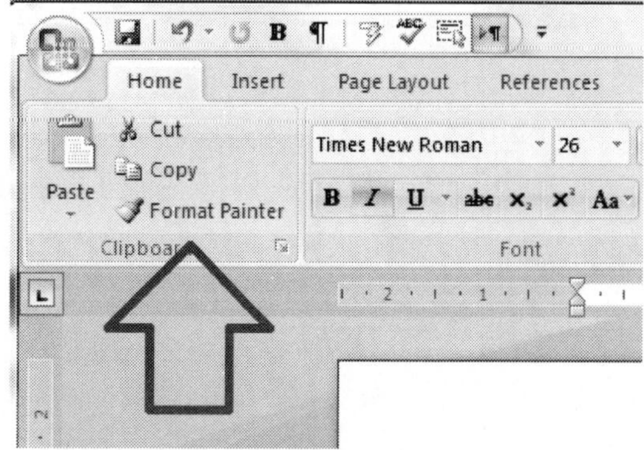

(a) Change background
(b) Highlight text
(c) Format painter
(d) Text color

21. The correct steps to insert line numbers in the margin alongside each line of the document is ______.
(a) Page layout tab → Page setup group → Section
(b) Page layout tab → Alignment group → Line numbers
(c) Page layout tab → Page setup group → Line numbers
(d) View tab → Paragraph → Line numbers

22. You can insert a hyperlink by.

(a) 

(b) 

(c) Alt + K

(d) MS Word does not support hyperlinks

23. You can use different page formats within the same document by separating the differently formatted area with a ______.
(a) Document break (b) Line break
(c) Section break (d) Format break

24. Which feature can you use to combine two or more cells into a single cell?
(a) Insert (b) Delete
(c) Merge (d) Split

25. Which of the following is NOT displayed on the status bar?
(a) Page number
(b) Number of words in a document
(c) Edit commands
(d) Zoom button

MS Paint

4

Chapter Outline:

- ❒ The Paint Window
- ❒ The Ribbon
- ❒ The Tools Menu
- ❒ Multiple Choice Questions

MS Paint is part of the Microsoft software used to make drawings and color them. It offers various options to add effects to your drawing.

The Paint Window

This is a typical view of the top of the Paint window.

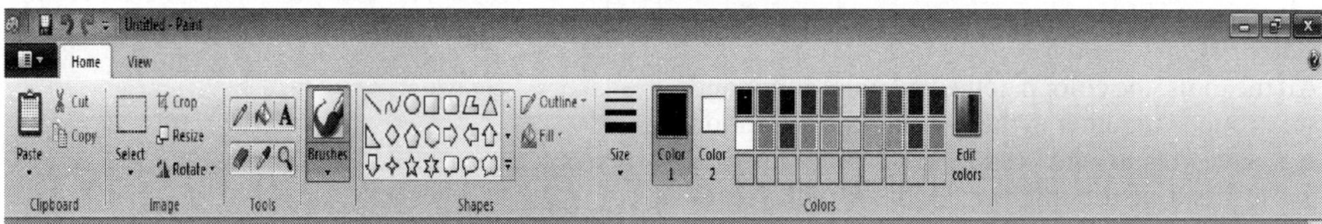

At the very top is the Title bar, just as in all programs, below it is a very simple Menu bar and below that is the **Ribbon**.

Title bar

At the left end of the Title bar, the first item shows a little paint palette. If clicked, this button opens a standard window menu, offering Restore, Move, Size, Minimise, Maximise and Close options.

Menu bar

The Menu bar has three items on the left and a Help button at the far right.

Paint button

First on the left is the **Paint button**, which opens a very comprehensive menu, similar to that shown here, plus a list of pictures you have recently saved.

Home tab

For nearly everything you do, you will want the **Home tab** to be at the front. The Home tab contains the Ribbon, from which tools and colors are selected. When you are making use of the View tab, you can flick back and forth between Home and View as often as you need to.

View tab

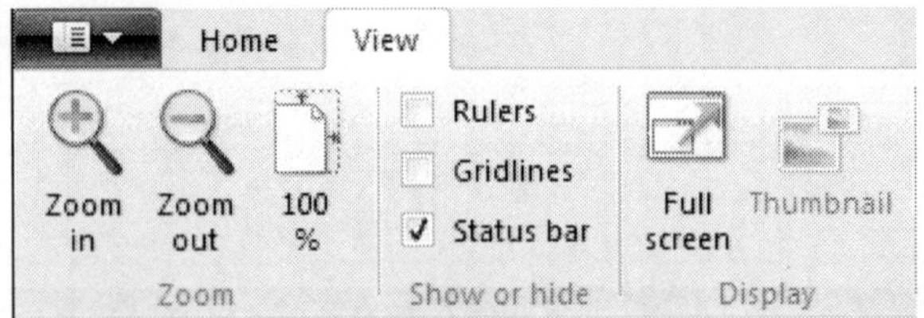

Zooming in and out is one of the features of Paint in Windows 7. **Zoom in** and **Zoom out** tools can be clicked repeatedly to get a closer or more distant view.

Ribbon

All the tools, the color palette, and most commands are grouped together in the ribbon. The exceptions are Save, Undo and Redo, which are shown at the left end of the title bar, in the **Quick Access Toolbar**.

Rectangular selection

Usually you will make a rectangular selection. After clicking the rectangular selection tool, position the cross-hair cursor at the top left part of the image or text you want to select, press your mouse button and drag down to its bottom right.

Selection options

To the right of the selection icon you will see three options, **Crop**, **Resize** and **Rotate flip**.

These will help you resize and change the orientation of your image.

Crop

The top button, a diamond shape with a line through it, lets you crop your picture so that only the selected area remains.

Resize and Skew

The second tiny button to the right of the large Select button will open the Resize and Skew dialog box.

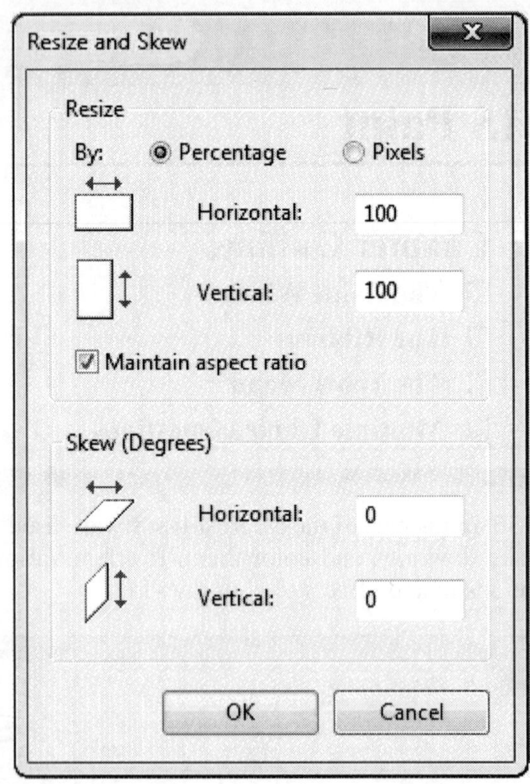

Drawing area

It is the area where you make your drawing with the help of a mouse.

Rotate or flip

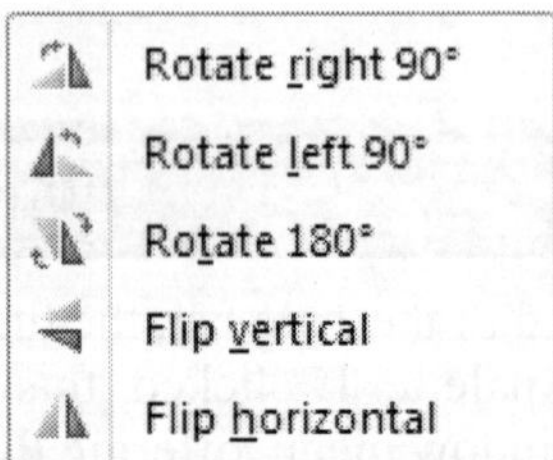

This menu lets you make mirror images of selections, either vertically or horizontally, and it also lets you rotate an item 90 degrees.

Tools menu

Pencil

The pencil tool can be used for free-hand drawing, or it can be used in a zoomed in view for pixel-by-pixel editing.

Fill with color

The Fill with color tool, or the Flood Fill tool, is used to fill **an area of a single color** with a different color. Color 1 will be used if you press the left mouse button on the area to be filled. Color 2 will be used if you press the right mouse button.

Brushes

Brushes let you paint in various widths and textures. Here we have drawn a line with each of the offered brushes, using the same color and the same line width for each. We have labelled each line according to its tool tip in the gallery.

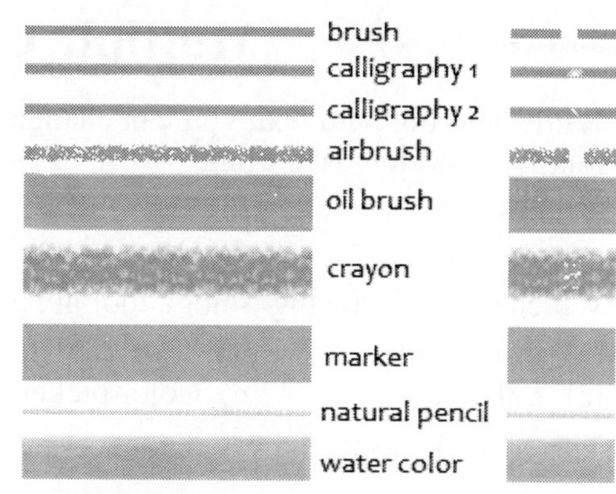

Color palette

The two top lines of the color palette show all the colors available.

Status bar

The Status bar sits at the very bottom of the Paint Window, where it offers information as you work.

Multiple Choice Questions

1. While working with text, you can change the font type and font size using _______.
   (a) Text pop-up (b) View menu
   (c) Text tab (d) Design box

2. Which of the following is not a tool in Paint?
   (a) Brush tool (b) Polish tool
   (c) Fill tool (d) Color picker

3. This menu is displayed when you _______.

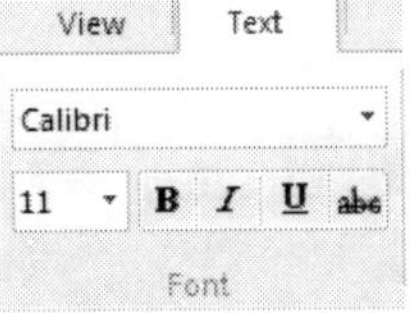

   (a) Click on **B** in the Home Tab of the ribbon
   (b) Select the text tool, and you select an area to enter text
   (c) Want to change the font size
   (d) All of these

4. What is the name of the tool used to fill a shape with colour called?
   (a) Colour tool
   (b) Fill tool
   (c) Fill color tool
   (d) Paint tool

5. The size of the image properties dialog box is not displayed in _______.
   (a) Inches
   (b) Pixels
   (c) Dots
   (d) Centimeters

6. Which of the following operations on text cannot be done using the Menu shown below?

View
Text
Calibri
11
B I U abc
Font

   (a) Bold
   (b) Italic
   (c) Superscript
   (d) Strikethrough

7. The image properties dialog box in MS Paint can also be used to set the colors. Which of the following options can be set in MS Paint?
   (a) Black and white, color
   (b) RGB, CMYK
   (c) Grayscale, Color
   (d) None of the above

8. In MS Paint, a picture can be skewed ______.
   (a) Only horizontally
   (b) Both horizontally and vertically
   (c) Only vertically
   (d) None of these

9. You can change the height and width of a picture using ______.
   (a) Image → Resize and Skew → Resize
   (b) Image → Resize and Skew → Flip Vertically
   (c) Paint Button → Width, Height
   (d) All of these

10. You can change the height and width of the drawing area using ______.
   (a) Image → Resize and Skew → Rotate 90°
   (b) Image → Resize and Skew → Flip Vertically
   (c) Paint Button → Properties → Width, Height
   (d) All of these

11. Which of the following operations would give an inverted mirror image of the picture?
   (a) Rotate 180° (b) Flip horizontal
   (c) Flip vertical (d) Rotate 90°

12. While creating the given image, the designer accidentally saved the image up-side down as shown in Image-I. Which operation should be used to correct the problem and show it in the correct direction as in Image-II?

Image-I **Image-II**

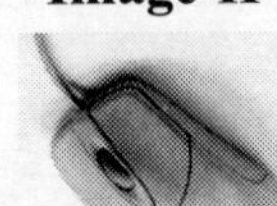

   (a) Rotate right 90° (b) Flip vertical
   (c) Skew (d) Flip horizontal

13. Which operation might have been performed to get Image-II from Image-I?

Image-I 

Image-II 

(a) Stretch
(b) Skew horizontal
(c) Skew vertical
(d) Flip vertical

14. Which of the following options is not a selection shape?

(a) 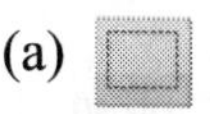 (b) 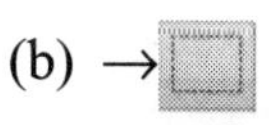
(c)  (d) 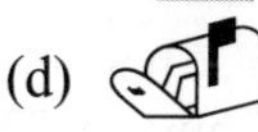

15. In MS Paint, which of the following options is used to view the drawing as it will look when printed?
(a) Print preview
(b) Page set up
(c) Print selected
(d) Page layout

16. Match the following.

Column-I	Column-II
(i) Skew	(a) To change the drawing to its mirror image
(ii) Thumbnail	(b) To rotate the drawing through a given angle
(iii) Bitmap	(c) To display the drawing in a small reference window
(iv) Flip	(d) File format to store Paint files

(a) (i)–(a), (ii)–(c), (iii)–(d), (iv)–(b)
(b) (i)–(a), (ii)–(d), (iii)–(c), (iv)–(b)
(c) (i)–(b), (ii)–(d), (iii)–(c), (iv)–(a)
(D) (i)–(b), (ii)–(c), (iii)–(d), (iv)–(a)

17. To draw a red circle with a blue boundary, you should set _____.
(a) Color 1 to blue, Color 2 to red and fill style to solid color
(b) Color 2 to blue, Color 1 to red and fill style to solid color
(c) Color 1 to first red and then blue, fill style to solid color
(d) You cannot draw such a circle with MS Paint

18. Match the following.

Column-I	Column-II
(i) No Fill	(a)
(ii) Natural Pencil	(b)
(iii) Solid Fill	(c)
(iv) Crayon	(d)

(a) (i)–(c), (ii)–(d), (iii)–(a), (iv)–(b)
(b) (i)–(c), (ii)–(d), (iii)–(b), (iv)–(a)
(c) (i)–(d), (ii)–(c), (iii)–(b), (iv)–(a)
(d) (i)–(d), (ii)–(c), (iii)–(a), (iv)–(b)

19. To draw a circle with no boundary, what should you do?

(a) Set the shape outline style to no outline
(b) Set the shape outline to solid Color
(c) Use the same Color1 and Color2
(d) None of these

20. Which of the following is not a shape outline style?
(a) Natural pencil
(b) Watercolor
(c) No outline
(d) No fill

Network

5

Chapter Outline:

- ❒ Types of Network
- ❒ Uses of Networks
- ❒ Multiple Choice Questions

Types of Network

A group of two or more computer systems together forms a computer network. It is used to transfer data from one device to another. It supports access to the world wide web, sending and receiving email, etc. A good example can be your computer lab.

There are the following three types of networks:

Local Area Network (LAN)

A local area network (LAN) is a computer network that connects computers within a limited area such as a home, school, computer laboratory, or office building, using network media. In other words, it provides the network connectivity only over a small geographic area.

HAN and SAN

HAN also called home area network and SAN also called storage area network are two types of LAN.

HAN is a type of local area network which facilitates communication among digital devices present inside or within the close vicinity of a home.

SAN is a dedicated network that provides access to consolidated data storage. SAN is used to enhance storage devices, such as disk arrays and tape libraries accessible to servers so that these devices appear locally attached to the operating system.

Wide Area Network (WAN)

A wide area network (WAN) is a network over a broad area. WAN is used by business and government organizations for exchange of information between employees, customers, clients and buyers. The Internet is an example of the largest and most effective WAN network.

WAN is very effective in connecting LANs so that users sitting and working in very far off places can easily share information over the network.

WANs are often built using leased lines. At each end of the leased line, a router connects the LAN on one side with a second router within the LAN on the other.

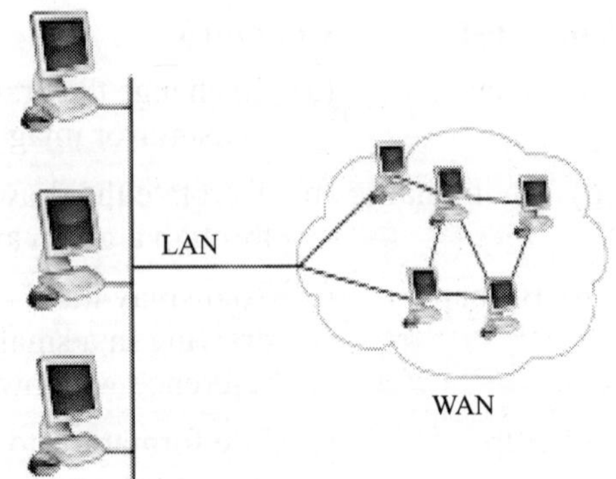

Uses of Networks

Networks are used for the following:

- Facilitating email, video conferencing, instant messaging services
- Enabling multiple users to share devices like a printer or scanner
- Enabling file sharing across the network
- Making information easily accesible

Multiple Choice Questions

1. This is the center of a computer network.
   (a) File server
   (b) Document
   (c) Control unit
   (d) Software

2. LAN stands for
   (a) Land Area Network
   (b) Local Arial Networking
   (c) Local Area Network
   (d) Load Assessment Network

3. Which is a popular networking software?
   (a) Unix
   (b) MS-Windows
   (c) Windows NT
   (d) All of these

4. Every computer in a network is called a ____.
   (a) Point
   (b) System
   (c) Node
   (d) None of these

5. WAN stands for ______.
   (a) Wide Area Network
   (b) World Area Network
   (c) World Arial Network
   (d) World Assessment Network

6. When a network of computers within a school are connected with cables, it is called ______.
   (a) LAN (b) WAN
   (c) MAN (d) None of these

7. A network where computers share data and programs over long distances across the world is called ______.
   (a) LAN (b) WAN
   (c) MAN (d) None of these

8. ______ converts digital signals to audible analog tones.
   (a) Converter (b) Modular
   (c) Transformer (d) Modem

9. A group of computers connected together is called a ______.
   (a) Station (b) Network
   (c) Port (d) Node

10. Where was the first ever Network setup?
    (a) USA (b) UK
    (c) India (d) Germany

11. What was the name of the first network?
    (a) EXTRANET
    (b) ARPANET
    (c) INTRANET
    (d) NET

12. Who set up the first network?
    (a) Department of Defense
    (b) Rupin Balua
    (c) Blaise Pascal
    (d) Roger Benjamin

13. When was the first ever network set up?
    (a) 1960 (b) 1969
    (c) 1962 (d) 1966

14. ______ acts a distributor of programs and data to be shared.
    (a) Server
    (b) Software
    (c) CPU
    (d) Mouse

15. A ______ is formed when two or more computers are connected to one another.
    (a) URL
    (b) Network
    (c) Hyperlink
    (d) Website

16. The ______ is a gigantic computer network that connects computers across the world.
    (a) Internet
    (b) World Wide Web
    (c) Intranet
    (d) Website

17. What are the advantages of networking?
    (a) Ease in transfer of data from one computer to another.
    (b) Ease in sharing printers amongst connected computers.
    (c) Easy sharing of Internet among connects computers.
    (d) All of these.

18. What type of network can be found in your school where computers within the computer laboratory and other departments are connected?
(a) School Area Network
(b) Local Area Network
(c) Metropolitan Area Network
(d) Wide Area Network

19. The networked computers send ______ back and forth amongst them.
(a) Data or information
(b) Electricity
(c) Cables
(d) None of the above

20. An end system connected to a network is generally called a ______.
(a) Host (b) PC
(c) Server (d) Modem

Internet and Its Uses

6

Chapter Outline:

- ❒ Blog or Web Log
- ❒ Internet
- ❒ Server
- ❒ URL
- ❒ Multiple Choicc Questions

Internet is a large group of computers connected to each other. It is also sometimes simply called the Net. No single individual or the government owns the internet. When two computers are connected over the Internet, they can send and receive all kinds of information.

Let us learn some technical terms to understand the usage of the internet clearly.

Blog or Web Log

A blog (short for "web log") is a type of web page that offers a series of posted items (short articles, photos, diary entries, etc.). A blog belongs to an individual who shares his ideas. The members of the blog can comment and share their opinions and ideas on the same.

Bookmarks/Favorites

All major web browsers include a way to store links to sites you wish to revisit. Netscape, Mozilla, and Firefox use the term Bookmarks. The equivalent in Internet Explorer (IE) is called a "Favorite." To create a bookmark, click on BOOKMARKS or FAVORITES, then ADD. To visit a bookmarked site, click on BOOKMARKS and click on the saved site from the list.

Browsers

Some software programs enable you to view web pages and other documents on the Internet. They "translate" HTML-encoded files into the text, images, sounds, and other features you see. The most commonly used browsers are Microsoft Internet Explorer (often called IE), Firefox, Mozilla, Safari, Opera and Chrome.

Cache

In browsers, "cache" is used to identify a space where web pages you have visited are stored in your computer.

Download

The download option on the browser or web page allows you to store the information for use any time later. Once downloaded, you can save the file in your secondary storage device, such as a pen drive. You can view this file whenever you want to without having to open the website again. To copy something from a primary source to a more peripheral one, as in saving something found on the Web (currently located on its server) to diskette or to a file on your local hard drive.

FTP

FTP refers to File Transfer Protocol. It is the ability to transfer rapidly entire files from one computer to another, intact, for viewing or other purposes.

History

It shows you the list of websites you have visited in the past. Available by using the combined keystrokes CTRL + H. You can set how many days your browser retains history in Edit → Preferences, or in Tools → Options.

HTML

Hypertext Markup Language is a standardized language of computer code, imbedded in "source" documents behind all Web documents, containing the textual content, images, links to other documents, etc.

Internet

The vast collection of interconnected networks that all use the TCP/IP protocols and that evolved from the ARPANET of the late 60s and early 70s.

An "internet" (lower case i) is any computers connected to each other (a network), and are not part of the Internet unless the use TCP/IP protocols.

An "intranet" is a private network inside a company or organization that uses the same kinds of software that you would find on the public Internet, but that is only for internal use.

IP address

Internet protocol address is a unique number consisting of 4 parts separated by dots, e.g., 155.112.245.4.

Every machine that is on the Internet has a unique IP address. If a machine does not have an IP number, it is not really on the Internet.

ISP or Internet Service Provider is a company that sells Internet connections. It is the internet service provider. Faster, more expensive Internet connectivity is available via cable or DSL.

Server or Web Server

A computer running that software is assigned an IP address and connected to the Internet so that it can provide documents via the World Wide Web.

Site or Web-Site

This term is often used to mean "web page," but there is a difference. A web page is a single entity, one URL, one file that you might find on the Web.

TCP/IP (Transmission Control Protocol/ Internet Protocol)

This is the suite of protocols that defines the Internet. Originally designed for the UNIX operating system, TCP/IP software is now available for every major kind of computer operating system. To be truly on the Internet, your computer must have TCP/IP software.

Telnet

Internet service allowing one computer to log onto another, connecting despite the remoteness of the computer, is the telnet.

URL

Uniform Resource Locator. The unique address of any Web document. It may be keyed in a browser's OPEN or LOCATION / GO TO box to retrieve a document. There is a logical layout of a URL:

Type of file (could say ftp:// or telnet://)	Domain name (computer file is on and its location on the Internet)	Path or directory on the computer to this file	Name of file, and its file extension (usually ending in .html or .htm)
http://	www.navneetmehra.edu/	Teaching/Tutor/ Navneet_M/	Finddetail.html

Multiple Choice Questions

1. The address of a website is known as _____. It is entered in the ______ bar of the browser window.
   (a) URL, hyperlinks
   (b) URL, hddress
   (c) Hyperlinks, address
   (d) Address, hyperlinks
2. What can you do using the Internet?
   (a) Download software
   (b) Participate in interactive forums
   (c) Chat with your friends
   (d) All of these
3. HTTP stands for ______.
   (a) Hypertext Transfer Protocol
   (b) Hyphentext Transfer Protocol
   (c) Hypertext Transfer Provider
   (d) Hypertransfer Text Protocol
4. The rule followed in the transmission of information on the Internet is called ______.
   (a) Internet Protocols
   (b) Internet Police
   (c) Interpol Police
   (d) Interpol Protocol
5. What all do you need to connect to the Internet?
   (a) Internet Service Provider
   (b) Modem
   (c) Software
   (D All of these
6. Internet service providers are the companies that give you access to the ______.
   (a) Documents (b) Files
   (c) Internet (d) Node
7. ______ is a piece of hardware that serves in exchanging information between two computers through the cables.
   (a) Wire (b) Modem
   (c) Scanner (d) None of these
8. A Client Program (software) that is used to look at various kinds of Internet resources is called a/an ______.
   (a) Address (b) Provider
   (c) Browser (d) Protocol
9. Web pages are written using ______.
   (a) Network (b) HTML
   (c) URL (d) Website
10. Which of the following is not a web browser?
    (a) Chrome
    (b) Mozilla
    (c) Internet explorer
    (d) Windows explorer
11. Which of the following is not an Indian ISP?
    (a) Verizon
    (b) Dishnet
    (c) Spectranet
    (d) Sify
12. Who developed the World Wide Web?
    (a) Sir Tim Berners-Lee
    (b) Taub-Schilling
    (c) Dennis Richie
    (d) Ronald Trump
13. How many types of modems are there?
    (a) 6 (b) 3
    (c) 4 (d) 5
14. Which of the following is not a search engine?
    (a) Alta vista
    (b) Excite
    (c) Meta Crawler
    (d) Orkut
15. Internet can be used for which of the following?
    (a) Buying and selling old and new goods
    (b) Checking exam results
    (c) Performing banking operations
    (d) All of these
16. The internet runs on a set of protocols called ______.
    (a) FTP (b) TCP/IP
    (c) HTTP (d) SMTP
17. What is FTP primarily used for?
    (a) Transferring files over the Internet
    (b) Sending secure e-mail messages
    (c) Establishing firewalls within networks
    (d) Routing fiber-optic connections

18. Which of the following is a popular website to view videos of latest songs and movies?

(a) facebook (b) YouTube

(c) Microsoft (d) skype

19. Internet is used for audio and video calling across geographies. A popular tool for such internet call is ______.

(a) skype (b) Google

(c) YAHOO! (d) ebY

20. Which of the following is a popular auction site on the internet?

(a) JABONG (b) amazon

(c) flipkart (d) ebY

21. Internet forums are commonly referred to as ______.

(a) Chat forums
(b) Discussion forums
(c) Mail forums
(d) Blogging forums

22. Your grandparents stay away from you. You want to make them happy. Which of the following can you do over the internet to make them happy without visiting them?

I. Ordering flowers for them and getting them delivered.
II. Seeing them on the computer
III. Sending the gifts
IV. Speaking with them
V. Baking cakes for them

(a) Only III and V (b) Only II and IV
(c) Only I (d) I, II, III and IV

23. Which of the following is not a social networking site?

(a) ibibo (b) facebook

(c) LinkedIn (d) Google

24. What does a URL beginning with "https://" indicate?

(a) You are viewing a sub domain
(b) You are visiting a secure website
(c) The webpage is running a server-side script
(d) The webpage is streaming data to your browser

25. Posting offensive messages online is also called ______.

(a) Spamming (b) Flaming
(c) Phishing (d) Phrasing

Windows 7

7

Chapter Outline:

- Home Group
- Windows Search
- Windows Taskbar
- Windows Touch
- Multiple Choice Questions

Windows 7 is an operating system developed by Microsoft. It is a part of the Windows NT family. The changes seen in this version of Windows are

- The taskbar shows biggest visual changes, where the old Quick Launch toolbar has been replaced with the ability to pin applications to taskbar.
- Buttons for pinned applications are integrated with the task buttons.
- Snap maximizes a window when it is dragged to the top of the screen.
- Windows 7 includes 13 additional sound schemes.

Windows 7 is available in six different editions.

Let us check out key features of Windows 7:

Home Group

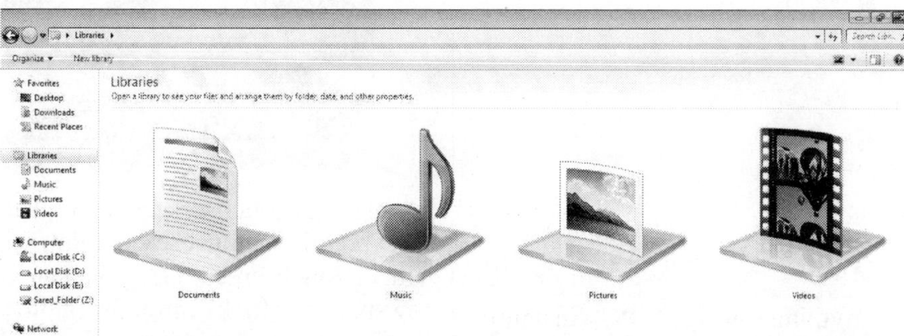

Takes the headache out of sharing files and printers on a home network. Now, you can easily connect two or more PCs running Windows 7 on your home network to automatically start sharing printers—and your media and document libraries—with other people in your home group.

Jump Lists

Speedy access to your favorite pictures, songs, websites, and documents. Jump Lists—new in Windows 7—take you right to the documents, pictures, songs, or websites you turn to each day. To open a Jump List, just right-click a program button on the Windows 7 taskbar.

Snap

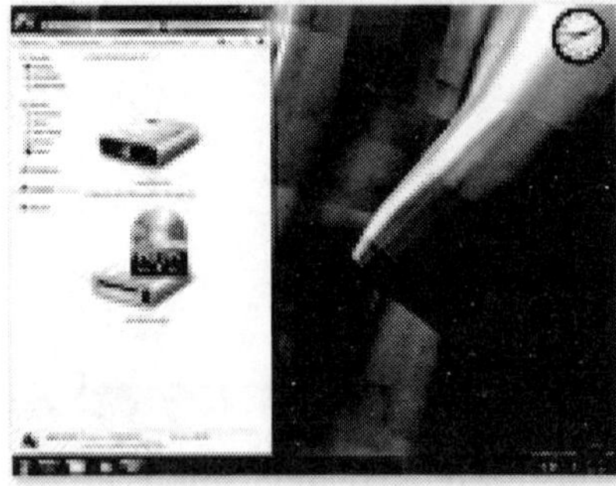

Snap is a quick (and fun) new way to resize open windows, simply by dragging them to the edges of your screen.

Windows Search

Find virtually anything on your PC, instantly. Start typing in the Start menu search box, and you will instantly see a list of relevant files on your PC. You can search by typing the name of the file, or based on its tags, file type, and even contents. To see even more matches, click a category in the results, like Documents or Pictures, or click See more results. Your search terms are highlighted to make it easier to scan the list.

Windows Taskbar

Better thumbnail previews, easier-to-see icons, and more ways to customize. The Show desktop button is a rectangular bar at the very end of the taskbar.

Windows Touch

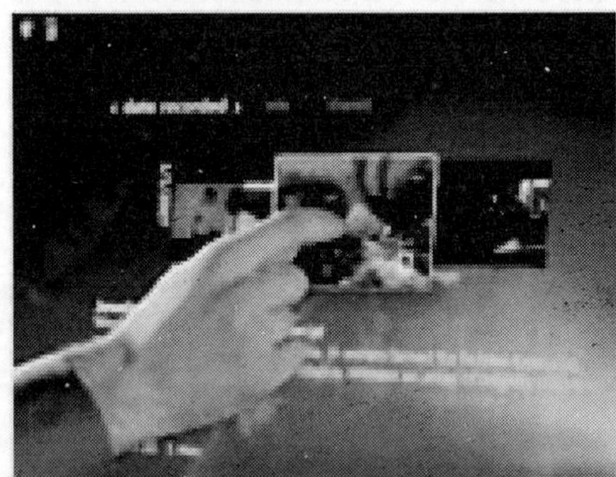

If you have a touchscreen, you will not always need a keyboard or mouse. When you pair Windows 7 with a touchscreen PC, you can browse online newspapers, flick through photo albums, and shuffle files and folders—using nothing but your fingers.

Limited one-finger touch capability has been available in Windows for years. But Windows 7 is the first to fully embrace multi-touch technology.

Multiple Choice Questions

1. What is Windows?
   (a) Database
   (b) Operating system
   (c) Programming language
   (d) Web-Based language
2. Who is the founder of Microsoft?
   (a) Charles Babbage
   (b) Bill Gates
   (c) Dennis Richie
   (d) Ronald Trump
3. What is the full form of GUI?
   (a) Graphic Utility Interface
   (b) Graphical User Integration
   (c) Graphical User Interface
   (d) Graphical Utility Integration
4. Identity the Icon.

   (a) Network (b) Computer
   (c) Recycle bin (d) Mozilla
5. The image displayed here is the image of the ______.

   (a) Windows explorer
   (b) Desktop
   (c) Control panel
   (d) Start menu
6.  represents _____.
   (a) Desktop
   (b) Start tab
   (c) Taskbar
   (d) Status
7. Which of the following is not present in control panel?
   (a) Programs
   (b) User accounts
   (c) Ease of access center
   (d) Windows media player
8. Which of the following modes is not present in 'Shut Down' menu of Start Button?
   (a) Hibernate
   (b) Sleep
   (c) Log in
   (d) Lock
9. Identify the icon here.

   (a) Action Center
   (b) Device Manager
   (c) Sound
   (d) Ease of Access Center
10. What is the shortcut to close a program?
    (a) Alt + F5
    (b) Alt + C
    (c) Alt + Esc
    (d) Alt + F4
11. The visual desktop experience that combines translucent windows, appealing color and graphic effects, and convenient functionally all comes in a group of features called ______.
    (a) Windows Aero
    (b) Graphical User Interface
    (c) Windows Tactile
    (d) Windows Experience
12. What will help you to exit a Window?
    (a) Open File Menu and click Exit
    (b) Click X on the upper right corner of the Window
    (c) Press Alt + F4
    (d) All of these

13. ______ put information and fun, like news, pictures, games and the phases of the moon, right on your desktop.
   (a) Apps
   (b) Accessories
   (c) Applications
   (d) Gadgets

14. To select your desktop's background and themes, you should ______.
   (a) Right click on desktop and click Personalize
   (b) Type Personalization in the Search Bar of the Start Menu.
   (c) Both (a) and (b)
   (d) None of these

15. When your desktop is cluttered with open windows, you can use ________ to select a single window and close the rest.
   (a) Peek (b) Shake
   (c) Steer (d) Flip

16. The Windows preview mode displayed in the given image is called _______.

   (a) Shake 3D
   (b) Clip 3D
   (c) Flip 3D
   (d) Peek 3D

17. The image here shows a mini-menu of performance tasks for an icon on the taskbar. This menu is called ______.

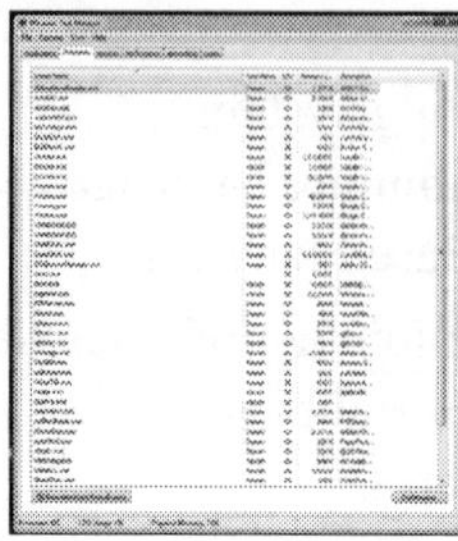

   (a) Jump List (b) Snap
   (c) Flip (d) Peek

18. When you scroll the mouse over the taskbar icons, a thumbnail preview of the open windows will appear as shown below. What is this view called?

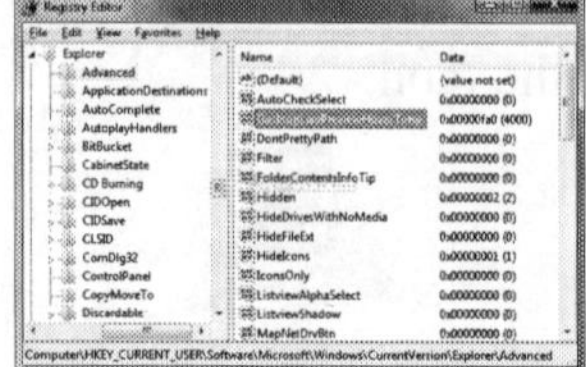

   (a) Snap (b) Peek
   (c) Flip (d) Shake

19. A Jump List on the taskbar does not allow a single access to _________.
   (a) Recent files
   (b) Remote desktops
   (c) Frequently viewed items
   (d) Performance tasks

20. What is the basic unit of storage that enables a computer to distinguish one set of information from another?
   (a) File (b) Folder
   (c) Data (d) Library

Latest Developments in IT

8

Chapter Outline:

- ❐ Phablet
- ❐ iTunes
- ❐ Multiple Choice Questions

Let us let us find out about the latest developments in the field of IT.

Phablet

The word phablet comes from phone and tablet. It is the latest addition to the field of IT. It comes with the features of both a smart phone and a tablet. Phablets have screens that measure approximately 5.1–6.9 inches. The popularity of phablets grew dramatically in 2012, after the success of the Galaxy note. The current largest 'commercially successful' phablet is the Sony Xperia Zultra with a 6.4" screen.

The advantages of using a phablet are:

- ♦ Bigger screens with better visibility
- ♦ Incredible cameras with better and faster autofocus
- ♦ Multitasking made easier as you can open many windows on its big screen

iTunes

iTunes is a media player library application developed by Apple Inc. It is used to play, download and organize audio and video files on personal computers with OS X and MicroSoft windows operating systems. The iTunes store is also available on the iphone and ipad.

Through the iTunes store, users can purchase and download music, music videos, television shows, audiobooks and podcasts movies.

iTunes 12 is the most recent major version of iTunes. It was released on October 16, 2014.

Multiple Choice Questions

1. What are the phablets?
   (a) They are a class of smart phones.
   (b) Their screen sizes range from 5″ to 6.9″ .
   (c) They combine the functionality of a tablet and a smart phone.
   (d) All of these.

2. What is bespoke software?
   (a) Old fashioned software
   (b) Multipurpose software
   (c) Custom software
   (d) General purpose software

3. What type of data is sent via SMS?
   (a) E-mail
   (b) Test messages
   (c) Facebook messages
   (d) Twitter updates

4. Which iPad apps let you see yourself in 3D before buying eye wear?
   (a) Glasses.com
   (b) Spectacles.com
   (c) Pulse.com
   (d) Eyewear.com

5. Which of the following is a popular VoIP application?
   (a) Google Chat (b) Skype
   (c) iPhone (d) Wifi Phone

6. This is a cloud storage and cloud computing service from Apple Inc. launched on October 12, 2011.
   (a) wCloud (b) iCloud
   (c) Cloud sync (d) eCloud

7. A word or a symbol prefixed with the symbol # used by services like Tumblr, Google+, etc is called a __________.
   (a) Google tag (b) Keyword
   (c) Search tag (d) Hashtag

8. Which of the following is a micro blogging and social networking service?
   (a) Wikipedia
   (b) Mozilla Firefox
   (c) Facebook
   (d) Mobile X

9. Kitkat is _____ version of Android operating system.
   (a) 4.2 (b) 4.4
   (c) 4.2 (d) 4.1

10. Identify the following:
    ♦ It is an app store.
    ♦ It is truly open and social.
    ♦ Billions of free downloads are being served by this app.
    (a) Mobile X (b) Mobility
    (c) Mobile9 (d) App9

11. Which of these is a Linux-based operating system designed primarily for touchscreen mobile devices such as smartphones and tablet computers?
    (a) Windows mobile
    (b) Symbian OS
    (c) iOS
    (d) Android

12. Which of the following Apple iOS was released on September 18, 2013?
    (a) iOS 8 (b) iOS 7
    (c) iOS 9 (d) iOS 6

13. What is the latest major release of the OS X for Apple INC's desktop and server Operating system for Macintosh computers called?
    (a) OS X Puma
    (b) OS X Snow Leopard
    (c) OS X Mavericks
    (d) OS X Mountain Lion

14. Which of these is a media player and media library application developed by Apple Inc?
    (a) Media Tunes
    (b) Siri
    (c) iTunes
    (d) Face Time

15. Which of the following apps helps you to share your app's installation directly with your friends?
    (a) Share app
    (b) Installed share app
    (c) Friends app
    (d) None of these

16. Which of the following is a free video chat service from Google that enables both one-on-one chats and group chats with up to ten people at a time?
(a) Google+ Nexus
(b) Google+ Chrome
(c) Google+ Hangouts
(d) Google+ Trends
17. What is the name of the Windows 8 tablet produced by Microsoft which was released on October 22, 2013?
(a) Surface (b) Courier
(c) iPad (d) Surface Pro 2
18. The slogan 'Loving it is easy. That's why so many people do' is used to promote ________.
(a) iPhone 1 (b) iPhone 4s
(c) iPhone 5 (d) iPhone 4
19. Which of the following I/O interfaces was most recently introduced?
(a) USB (b) FireWire
(c) Thunderbolt (d) eSATA
20. What is the name of Google's mobile operating system?
(a) Window's Mobile
(b) Chrome
(c) iOS
(d) Android
21. Which memory card format is most widely used?
(a) Compact Flash (CF)
(b) Secure Digital (SD)
(c) SmartMedia
(d) Memory stick
22. What is the default operating system for Macintosh Computers?
(a) Mac OS X (b) Apple OS
(c) iOS (d) Windows
23. What technology allows you to receive messages without checking your e-mail?
(a) Push (b) Pull
(c) Drive (d) Sweep
24. What is the distinguished characteristic of a retina display?
(a) 3D video support
(b) High resolution
(c) Reduced eye fatigue
(d) A built in camera
25. Google docs can be categorized as what type of software?
(a) Shareware
(b) Vaporware
(c) Commercial software
(d) Software as a Service (SaaS)

SECTION 2
LOGICAL REASONING

Patterns

1

Chapter Outline:

- ❒ Odd One Out
- ❒ Complete The Two Words
- ❒ Matching Pairs
- ❒ Series
- ❒ Multiple Choice Questions

In questions on patterns you need to identify the logic of a pattern or series and accordingly continue that logic to arrive at the solution. This type of question may include problems on choosing odd one out, completing a of series, matching pairs, etc.

Odd One Out

As the name suggests, odd one out questions ask you to pick out thc one which is different from the other given options. All the others will follow the same kind of pattern except one. Following examples will make it clear.

Example: Find the odd one out.

(a) EHG (b) JML

(c) UYX (d) TWV

Answer: Option (c)

The pattern is: there is a gap of one letter, which is between the first and third letter. 2nd letter is the one that comes after the 3rd letter.

(i) E(F)HG

(ii) J(K)ML

(iii) Should be U(V)XW

(iv) T(U)WV

Example: Find the odd one out.

(a) 53 (b) 33

(c) 43 (d) 83

Answer: Option (b)

53, 43, 83 are prime number and 33 is divisible by 3 and 11.

Complete The Two Words

In this type, you will have to find the letter which forms the last letter of a word and also forms the first letter of another word. Following examples will make it clear.

Example: Find the letter which will end the first word and start the second word.

MAS?ING

(a) A (b) G

(c) Q (d) K

Answer: Option (d)

The answer is K because it completes the first word as MASK and also begins the second word as KING.

Matching Pairs

In this type, you will see one alphabet/number matches to other in some pattern. Following the same pattern you have to find the equivalent pair of given combination. Following examples will make it clear.

Alphabet matching:

Example: Find the matching pair.

MZ is to LY as KK is to?

(a) JA (b) HI

(c) JW (d) GB

Answer: Option (c)

MZ: In LY, the first letter L in the secound group of letters is the letter that comes before the first letter of the first group of letters M. Similarly, second letter in the second group, i.e Y, is the letter that comes before second letter in the first group. Similarly, KK: JW.

Number matching:

Example: Find the matching pair.

252 is to 5 as 343 is to?

(a) 5 (b) 4

(c) 8 (d) 3

Answer: Option (b)

252: 5 follows the pattern that the 2nd digit is the solution i.e 2(5)2. Similarly 3(4)3 is to 4.

Series

In this type of questions, there is a series of letters/ numbers and you have to understand the pattern followed and accordingly find the next letter in the series. Following examples will make it clear.

Example: Find the next letter in the series.

Z Y W T P K?

(a) A (b) N

(c) E (d) D

Answer: Option (c)

The answer is E, because the pattern is to count backwards from the first given letter: first one, then two, then three, then four, then five and lastly six.

Example: Find the missing pair of letters in the series.

FA, EC, DE, CG,?

(a) WE (b) CZ

(c) DI (d) BI

Answer: Option (d)

The answer is BI, because the pattern is to count backwards in ones for the first letter, and count forwards in two words for the second letter.

First letter FA EC DE CG B

Second letter FA EC DE CG BI

Multiple Choice Questions

1. Find the odd one out.
   (a) DE (b) GH
   (c) LM (d) ON
2. Find the odd one out.
   (a) BDC (b) EGF
   (c) HIJ (d) NPO
3. Find the odd one out.
   (a) RQ (b) NM
   (c) JI (d) PQ
4. Find the odd one out.
   (a) XZ (b) VW
   (c) ST (d) PQ
5. Find the odd one out.
   (a) ZYX (b) WVU
   (c) LMC (d) TSR
6. Find the odd one out.
   (a) 234 (b) 345
   (c) 456 (d) 657
7. Find the odd one out.
   (a) 654 (b) 765
   (c) 534 (d) 876
8. Find the odd one out.
   (a) 3445 (b) 4556
   (c) 7889 (d) 5567
9. Find the odd one out.
   (a) 3211 (b) 75444
   (c) 2100 (d) 5433
10. Find the odd one out.
    (a) 12321 (b) 1331
    (c) 121 (d) 12341
11. Find the odd one out.
    (a) Roof (b) Leaves
    (c) Stem (d) Plant
12. Find the odd one out.
    (a) Book (b) Pencil
    (c) Paper (d) Maths
13. Find the odd one out.
    (a) Bus (b) Car
    (c) Jeep (d) Cycle
14. Find the odd one out.
    (a) Walk (b) Sail
    (c) Ride (d) Drive
15. Find the odd one out.
    (a) Staircase (b) Bridge
    (c) Ladder (d) Escalator

Directions for questions 16 to 25: Find the letter that is most suited.

16. BE?AS
    (a) T (b) G
    (c) Y (d) R
17. BOT?URT
    (a) L (b) O
    (c) H (d) P
18. SHAR?RINT
    (a) P (b) K
    (c) T (d) Y
19. CAME?IGHT
    (a) R (b) L
    (c) P (d) K
20. HAN?ATE
    (a) K (b) P
    (c) D (d) L
21. SAL?ILL
    (a) T (b) K
    (c) P (d) N
22. MA?ET
    (a) K (b) T
    (c) N (d) L
23. DUC?ITE
    (a) Y (b) L
    (c) R (d) K
24. MAT?VER
    (a) O (b) E
    (c) S (d) C
25. RUI?EAR
    (a) N (b) K
    (c) T (d) B

Directions for questions 26 to 40: Find the pair of letters that is most suited.

26. FB is to GD as PM is to
    (a) RO (b) SP
    (c) RN (d) QO
27. NA is to LF as XN is to
    (a) YS (b) VS
    (c) YM (d) WM
28. FH is to DF as UV is to
    (a) SW (b) TX
    (c) RX (d) TW
29. KM is to OJ as VH is to
    (a) AG (b) YF
    (c) ZE (d) YG
30. DI is to EE as RQ is to
    (a) QN (b) TO
    (c) PP (d) SM
31. GH is to KL as PQ is to
    (a) ST (b) TU
    (c) UV (d) UT
32. CK is to KS as MU is to
    (a) UC (b) CU
    (c) BT (d) TB
33. YW is to VT as NL is to
    (a) IK (b) JH
    (c) KI (d) HJ
34. DH is to KO as RV is to
    (a) CY (b) BZ
    (c) ZB (d) YC
35. FG is to JK as NO is to
    (a) TU (b) UT
    (c) RT (d) RS
36. JK is to NA as QH is to
    (a) SM (b) UL
    (c) TS (d) SL
37. NT is to HP as WE is to
    (a) QA (b) BY
    (c) SB (d) SA
38. XL is to XF as YP is to
    (a) ED (b) ZJ
    (c) YJ (d) EP
39. 4 is to 16 as 16 is to
    (a) 72 (b) 64
    (c) 60 (d) 33
40. 3 is to 12 as 12 is to
    (a) 24 (b) 48
    (c) 36 (d) 25

Directions for questions 41 to 50: Find the next letter/number in the series

41. X W V U T ?
    (a) Q (b) R
    (c) S (d) P
42. W V T Q M ?
    (a) I (b) H
    (c) G (d) K
43. A B E J Q ?
    (a) W (b) X
    (c) Y (d) Z
44. Z Y V Q J ?
    (a) A (b) B
    (c) C (d) D
45. I J H K G ?
    (a) E (b) F
    (c) L (d) M
46. T Y C F H ?
    (a) J (b) I
    (c) K (d) L
47. 4 5 7 10 14 ?
    (a) 21 (b) 18
    (c) 19 (d) 20
48. 27 25 22 18 13 ?
    (a) 7 (b) 5
    (c) 9 (d) 3
49. 49 58 67 76 85 ?
    (a) 91 (b) 92
    (c) 93 (d) 94
50. 800 400 200 100 50 ?
    (a) 15 (b) 20
    (c) 25 (d) 30

Analogy and Classification

2

Chapter Outline:

- Analogy
- Classification
- Multiple Choice Questions

Analogy

Analogy means similarity. Analogy specifies a relationship between given words, events, objects or alphabet sets which has to be recognised. In this type of question, two terms/figures related in some way are given and the third term/figure is also given with four or five alternatives. The answer is reached by the process of reasoning on the basis of parallel events or objects.

Example: 'College' is related to 'Teachers' in the same way as 'Hospital' is related to:

(a) Doctors
(b) Patients
(c) Medicine
(d) Beds

Answer: Option (a)

As teaching is done by 'Teachers' in the 'College' similarly treatment is done by 'Doctors' in the 'Hospital'.

Example: 'Flower' is related to 'Bud' in the same way as 'Fruit' is related to:

(a) Seed (b) Tree
(c) Flower (d) Stem

Answer: Option (c)

As 'Flower' is made from 'Bud' similarly 'Fruit' is made from 'Flower'.

Example: 4 : 18 :: 6 : ?

(a) 32 (b) 38
(c) 11 (d) 37

Answer: Option (b)

As, $(4)^2 + 2 = 18$

Similarly, $(6)^2 + 2 = 38$.

Classification

In classification, a set of terms/figures is given in which all (except one) follow similar properties. You have to identify the property followed in the set and find the odd one out.

Example: Glove : Hand :: ? : ?

(a) Neck : Collar
(b) Tie : Shirt
(c) Socks : Feet
(d) Coat : Pocket

Answer: Option (c)

As gloves are worn in hands similarly socks are worn on feet.

Example: Letter : Word :: ? : ?

(a) Page : Book
(b) Product : Factory
(c) Club : People
(d) Home work : School

Answer: Option (a)

As word is a group of letters similarly book is a group of pages.

Multiple Choice Questions

1. Sword is related to Slaughter in the same way as Scalpel is related to
   (a) Murder (b) Stab
   (c) Surgery (d) Chopping
2. Life is related to Autobiography in the same way as Witness is related to
   (a) Papers (b) Truth
   (c) Documents (d) Acceptance
3. Chef is related to Restaurant in the same way as Druggist is related to
   (a) Medicine (b) Pharmacy
   (c) Store (d) Chemist
4. Jade is related to Green in the same way as Garnet is related to
   (a) Blue (b) Orange
   (c) Red (d) Yellow
5. Dancer is related to Stage in the same way as Priest is related to
   (a) Pulpit (b) Assembly
   (c) Parliament (d) State
6. Birds are related to Aviary in the same way as Bees are related to
   (a) Aquarium (b) Hive
   (c) Brewery (d) Apiary
7. Resign is related to Politician in the same way as Abdicate is related to
   (a) Prince (b) King
   (c) Realm (d) Throne
8. Scissors are related to Cloth in the same way as Scythe is related to
   (a) Wood (b) Steel
   (c) Grass (d) Paper
9. Gardener is related to Trowel in the same way as Seamstress is related to
   (a) Saw (b) Scissors
   (c) Sneakers (d) Crowbar
10. Prose is related to Writing in the same way as Lisp is related to
    (a) Reading (b) Music
    (c) Speech (d) Drawing
11. Estonia is related to Rouble in the same way as Chile is related to
    (a) Dinar (b) Peso
    (c) Peseta (d) Franc
12. Engineer is related to Machine in the same way as Doctor is related to
    (a) Hospital (b) Body
    (c) Disease (d) Medicine
13. Neck is related to Tie in the same way as Waist is related to
    (a) Watch (b) Belt
    (c) Ribbon (d) Shirt
14. Oriya is related to Odisha in the same way as Dogri is related to
    (a) Himachal Pradesh (b) Sikkim
    (c) Jammu (d) Assam
15. Satyajit is related to Films in the same way as Picasso is related to
    (a) Literature (b) Drama
    (c) Poetry (d) Painting
16. South is related to North-West in the same way as West is related to
    (a) South-West (b) East
    (c) North-East (d) South
17. Bull is related to Draught in the same way as Cow is related to
    (a) Livestock (b) Milch
    (c) Farm (d) Fodder
18. Summit is related to Apex in the same way as Summon is related to
    (a) Court (b) Judge
    (c) Witness (d) Backon
19. Distil is related to Whisky in the same way as Brew is related to
    (a) Ferment (b) Gin
    (c) Beer (d) Sugar
20. DDT is related to Abbreviation in the same way as LASER is related to
    (a) Antithesis (b) Acronym
    (c) Epigram (d) Epithet

❖❖❖

Coding and Decoding

3

Chapter Outline:

- ❒ Letter Coding
- ❒ Multiple Choice Questions

A CODE is a 'system of signals'. Therefore, Coding is a method of transmitting a message between the sender and the receiver without a third person knowing it. Decoding is the process of understanding a code language.

Letter Coding

In letter coding type of questions, the real letters in a word are replaced by certain other letters according to a specific rule to form its code. You are required to detect the common rule and answer the questions accordingly.

Example: In the following questions, some capital letters (alphabet) are written in a row and below them their coding has been given. Study the table below and answer the given questions.

A	C	D	F	H	I	J	E	R	O	M	N	T	U
a	D	3	5	b	6	C	d	f	h	t	u	8	9

Find the code for 'CHATUR'

(a) Dba89d (b) Dba89f

(c) D98ab1 (d) Dba98f

Answer: Option (b)

Observe the table and take the code for each letters so, the code for CHATUR is 'dba89f'

Example: If in certain language, MADRAS is code as NBESBT, how is BOMBAY coded in that language?

(a) CPNCBX (b) CPNCBZ

(c) CPOCBZ (d) CQOCBZ

Answer: (b)

Each letter in the word is moved one step forward to obtain the corresponding letter of the code.

$M + 1 \Rightarrow N$ So, $B + 1 \Rightarrow C$

$A + 1 \Rightarrow B$ $O + 1 \Rightarrow P$

$D + 1 \Rightarrow E$ $M + 1 \Rightarrow N$

$R + 1 \Rightarrow S$ $B + 1 \Rightarrow C$

$A + 1 \Rightarrow B$ $A + 1 \Rightarrow B$

$S + 1 \Rightarrow T$ $Y + 1 \Rightarrow Z$

Example: If DOWN is code as FQYP, then how is the word WITH coded in that language?

(a) KYJN (b) IJYK

(c) YKVJ (d) JKVY

Answer: Option (c)

The letters of the word are moved two steps for word

D + 2 = F; O + 2 = Q; W + 2 = Y; N + 2 = P. Similarly, W + 2 = Y; I + 2 = K; T + 2 = V; H + 2 = J.

Example: If CHAIR is coded as FKDLU, then what is the code of RAID?

(a) ULGD (b) ULKG

(c) ULDG (d) UDLG

Answer: Option (d)

The word is coded by moving each letter three steps forward.

C H A I R + 3 = F K D L U. Similarly, R A I D + 3 = U D L G

Multiple Choice Questions

Directions for questions 1 to 10: Under each capital letter, a small letter is written, which is to be used as a code for the capital letter.

Letter	A	B	C	D	E	F	G	H	I	J	K	L,	M
Code	e	b	n	f	Y	l	h	i	p	a	k	w	v

Letter	N	O	P	Q	R	S	T	U	V	W	X	Y	Z
Code	u	b	z	c	Q	d	o	r	s	t	j	m	G

Group of four capital letters and their equivalent codes are given in column II respectively.

Match the following.

Column I	Column II
1. J D R U	(a) a e g i
2. C V F O	(b) v y r j
3. M F H B	(c) n f b k
4. J A Z H	(d) t a d i
5. Q U N T	(e) c y b r
6. W E S T	(f) a f q r
7. C D O K	(g) n s l b
8. M E U X	(h) t y d o
9. Q E O U	(i) c r u o
10. W J S F	(j) v l i b

Directions for questions 11 to 15: If MEGHA is coded as NFHIB and PEARL is coded as QFBSM, then

11. Identify the code for VIHANG.
    (a) WJIBOI (b) WJIOBH
    (c) WIJBHO (d) WJIBOH
12. Identify the code for BHOOMI.
    (a) CIPQNI (b) CINPPJ
    (c) CIPPNJ (d) ICPPNJ
13. Identify the code for PRABHA.
    (a) QSBCIB (b) QSBCBI
    (c) QQBCIB (d) QSBCCI
14. Identify the code for AKHILESH.
    (a) BLIJMFTT (b) BLIJFMTI
    (c) BILJMFTI (d) BLIJMFTI
15. Identify the code for FAMILY.
    (a) GBNJMW (b) GBNJMZ
    (c) GBNMJVV (d) GBMWMJ

Directions for questions 16 to 20: If VRUNDA is coded as XTWPFC and SWEETU is coded as UYGGVW, then

16. Identify the code for RAKESH.
    (a) TCMGOJ (b) TCMGUJ
    (c) TCMJUG (d) TCMGUT
17. Identify the code for VARSHA.
    (a) XTCUJT (b) XCTUJC
    (c) XTCUJC (d) CTXUJC
18. Identify the code for THERMAL.
    (a) VJGTOCN (b) JVGTOCN
    (c) VJGOTCN (d) CTXUJC
19. Identify the code for CHINTU.
    (a) EJKPVW (b) EKJPVW
    (c) EKPVWI (d) FKLQWX
20. Identify the code PINTU.
    (a) RKPVW (b) RKVPW
    (c) PKRVW (d) RKPWN

Alphabet and Ranking Test

4

Chapter Outline:

- ❒ **Alphabet Test**
- ❒ **Ranking Test**
- ❒ **Multiple Choice Questions**

Alphabet Test

In alphabet test questions, certain words are given. The candidate is required to arrange them in the order in which they shall be arranged in a dictionary and then state the word which is placed in the desired place. For such questions, the candidate requires basic knowledge of the 'Dictionary Usage'. In a dictionary, the words are put in alphabetical order with respect to the second alphabet of the words and so on.

Ranking Test

In ranking-based problems, usually the ranks of one or two persons from the top and from the bottom are mentioned. A candidate is required to compute either the total number of persons or rank of a particular person.

Example: Aarti scored more than Golu. Yash scored as much as Asha. Latika scored less than Manju. Golu scored more than Yash. Manju scored less than Asha. Who scored the highest?

(a) Manju (b) Yash
(c) Latika (d) Golu

Students scored in ascending order as follows

Aarti > Golu > Yash = Asha > Manju > Latika

Aarti scores the highest.

Study the following alphabet series to solve the exercise.

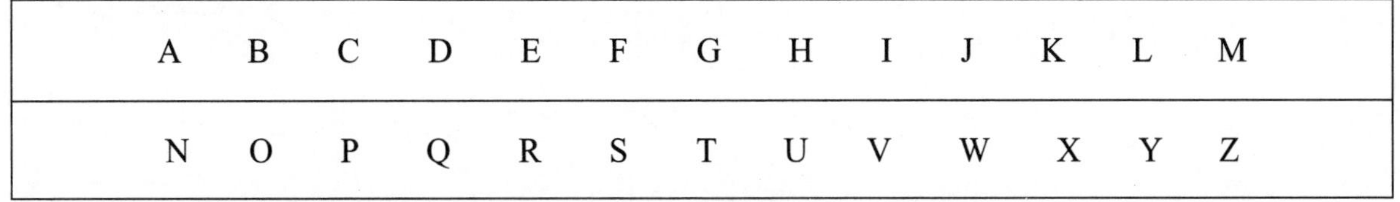

A	B	C	D	E	F	G	H	I	J	K	L	M
N	O	P	Q	R	S	T	U	V	W	X	Y	Z

Example: Which letter is exactly in the middle between E and K?

(a) G (b) H
(c) I (d) J

Answer: Option (b)

Write all the letters from 'E' to 'K'

E F G H I J K

So, the letter in the middle of 'E' and 'K' is 'H'

Example: Which letter is on right side of Q?

(a) P (b) O
(c) S (d) R

Answer: Option (d)

The letter to the right side of 'Q' means the letter which comes next to Q, i.e.'R'.

So, answer is option (d).

Example: Which letter is on the left side of P?

(a) O (b) N
(c) Q (d) S

Answer: Option (a)

The letter just on the left side of 'P' means the letter which comes before' P', i.e. 'O'.

So, answer is option (a)

Example: Which letter is at the 9th place from the left?

(a) Q (b) R
(c) H (d) I

Answer: Option (d)

9th letter from the left means 9th letter from the first, i.e. 'I'.

(A B C D E F G H I J K........)

So, the answer is option D.

Example: Which letter occurs twice in PARTICULARLY, but only once in TERRIBLE?

(a) R (b) L
(c) A (d) I

Answer: Option (b)

The letter A, R and L occur twice in PARTICULARLY.

The answer is L, because it appears twice in PARTICULARLY and once in TERRIBLE.

(Not A, because there are no As in the second word.)

(Not R, because there are 2 Rs in the second word.)

Example: Which letter is exactly between the first half of the alphabet?

(a) F (b) H
(c) G (d) I

Answer: Option (c)

There are 26 letters in the English alphabet. The first half are 13 in number, i.e, from A to M.

A B C D E F G H I J K L M

The 7th letter is exactly between A and M.

7th letter is 'G'.

Multiple Choice Questions

1. Which letter is exactly between R and V?
   (a) S (b) U
   (c) T (d) I
2. Which letter is exactly in the middle of the English alphabet?
   (a) M (b) N
   (c) L (d) No letter
3. Raju is sixth from the left end and Viru is tenth from the right end in a row of boys. If there are eight boys between Raju and Viru, how many boys are there in the row?
   (a) 24 (b) 26
   (c) 23 (d) 25
4. A class of boys stands in a single line, one boy is 19th in order from both the ends, How many boys are there in the class?
   (a) 37 (b) 39
   (c) 27 (d) 38
5. Sameer ranked 9th from the top and 38th from the bottom in a class. How many students are there in the class?
   (a) 45 (b) 47
   (c) 46 (d) 48
6. Which group of letters in its number position is at interval of 6?
   (a) GMSX (b) IOTZ
   (c) FLRX (d) GKQR
7. If every alternate letter in the alphabet is deleted, then how many letters will be left in the alphabet?
   (a) 12 (b) 13
   (c) 14 (d) 15
8. If Tuesday falls on 4th of the month, then which day will be three days after the 24th?
   (a) Monday (b) Tuesday
   (c) Friday (d) Thursday
9. If 30th January 2003 was Thursday, what was the day on 2nd March 2003?
   (a) Sunday
   (b) Thursday
   (c) Tuesday
   (d) Saturday
10. If first day of the year (not a leap year) was Monday, then what was the last day of the year?
    (a) Friday
    (b) Saturday
    (c) Monday
    (d) Sunday
11. Which letter occurs twice in INDIA and twice in BRITAIN?
    (a) T (b) D
    (c) I (d) N
12. Which letter occurs twice in SUPPORTER, but only once in OVERTAKE?
    (a) E (b) R
    (c) P (d) E
13. How many days will be there from 26th January 2008 to 15th May 2008 (both days included)?
    (a) 111 (b) 112
    (c) 110 (d) 113
14. If the day before yesterday was Thursday, when will Sunday be?
    (a) Tomorrow
    (b) Today
    (c) Day after tomorrow
    (d) None of these
15. Which letter occurs once in GINGER, twice in BEGINNER but not at all in DIVIDE?
    (a) D (b) N
    (c) G (d) E
16. How many 4s are there preceded by 7 but not followed by 3?
    5 9 3 2 1 7 4 2 6 9 7 4 6 1 3 2 8 7 4 1 3 8 3 2 5 6 7 4 3 9 5 8 2 0 1 8 7 4 6 3
    (a) Four (b) Three
    (c) Six (d) Five
17. How many combinations of two-digit numbers having 8 can be made from the following numbers?
    8, 5, 2, 1, 7, 6
    (a) 10 (b) 6
    (c) 9 (d) 11

18. If the first half of the alphabet is written backwards, which letter is in the13th position?
(a) B (b) C
(c) A (d) L

19. 517 325 639 841 792
What will be the first digit of the second highest number after the positions of the 2nd and 3rd digits within each number are interchanged?
(a) 8 (b) 2
(c) 7 (d) 9

20. If day after tomorrow is Saturday, what day was 3 days before yesterday?
(a) Monday (b) Sunday
(c) Tuesday (d) Thursday

21. How many numbers amongst the numbers 9 to 54 are there which are exactly divisible by 9 but not by 3?
(a) 5 (b) 6
(c) 0 (d) 9

22. Which letter occurs twice in POMEGRANATE, twice in PINEAPPLE, but only once in PROPERLY?
(a) N (b) P
(c) A (d) E

23. Which letter occurs twice in IMITATE, twice in INTENSION and once in INTERIOR?
(a) I (b) R
(c) E (d) T

24. If the position of the first and sixth digits of the number 2796543018 are interchanged, similarly the positions of the second and seventh digits are interchanged and so on, which of the following will be the left of seventh digit from the left end?
(a) 1 (b) 7
(c) 0 (d) 8

25. If it is possible to form a number which is a perfect square of a two-digit odd number using the second, fourth, seventh digits of the number 739142658 using each only once, which of the following is the second digit of that two-digit odd number?
(a) 4 (b) 7
(c) 3 (d) None of these

26. Which is the third number to the left of the number which is exactly in the middle of the following sequence of numbers?
1 2 3 4 5 6 7 8 9 2 4 6 8 9 7 5 3 1 9 8 7 6 5 4 3 2 1
(a) 3 (b) 5
(c) 4 (d) 7

27. In the following series of numbers, how many 1, 3, 7 have appeared together. 7 being in middle and 1, 3 on either side?
2 9 7 3 1 7 3 7 7 1 3 3 1 7 3 8 5 7 1 3 7 7 1 7 3 9 0 6
(a) 4 (b) 5
(c) 3 (d) More than 5

28. If the following series is written in the reverse order, which number will be fourth to the right of the seventh number from the left?
7, 3, 9, 7, 0, 3, 8, 4, 6, 2, 1, 0, 5, 11, 13
(a) 5 (b) 11
(c) 9 (d) 0

29. Which letter occurs twice in the three words of the above question?
(a) I (b) I, T
(c) I, N (d) R, N, T

30. Which letter occurs in IDEA and not in IDLE, but exists in DEAL?
(a) L (b) A
(c) D (d) I

❖❖❖

Direction Sense Test

5

Chapter Outline:

- ❒ Key Points on Directions
- ❒ Multiple Choice Questions

There are four main directions. They are East, West, North and South. These directions are also called cardinal directions.

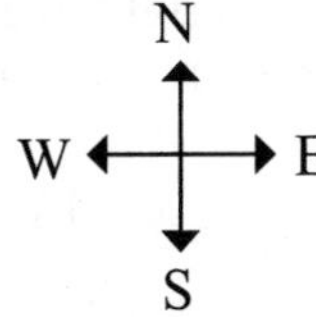

There are four intermediate directions. They are North-East (N-E), North-West (N-W), South-East (S-E), and South-West (S-W) as shown below:

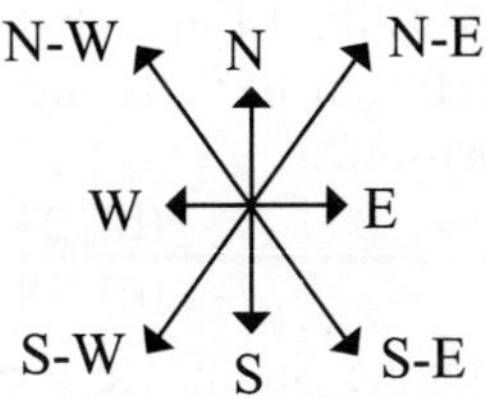

Key Points on Directions

1. At the time of sunrise if a man stands facing the east, his shadow will be towards west.
2. At the time of sunset, the shadow of an object is always in the east.
3. If a man stands facing the North, at the time of sunrise his shadow will be towards his left and at the time of sunset it will be towards his right.
4. At 12:00 noon, the rays of the sun are vertically downward, hence there will be no shadow.

Multiple Choice Questions

1. A river flows west to east and on the way turns left and goes in a semi-circle around a hillock, and then turns left at right angles. In which direction is the river finally flowing?
   (a) West (b) East
   (c) North (d) South

2. I am facing south. I turn right and walk 20 m. Then I turn right again and walk 10 m. Then I turn left and walk 10 m and then turning right walk 20 m. Then I turn right again and walk 60 m. In which direction am I from the starting point?
   (a) North (b) North-West
   (c) East (d) North-East

3. A rat runs 20 ft towards the East and turns right, runs 10 ft and turns right, runs 9 ft and again turns left, runs 5 ft and then turns left, runs 12 ft and finally turns left and runs 6 ft. Now, in which direction is the rat facing?
   (a) East (b) West
   (c) North (d) South

4. Starting from a point P, Sachin walked 20 m towards South. He turned left and walked 30 m. He then turned left and walked 20 m. He again turned left and walked 40 m and reached a point Q. How far and in which direction is the point Q from the point P?
   (a) 20 m West (b) 10 m East
   (c) 10 m North (d) None of these

5. Rohan walks a distance of 3 Km towards North, then turns to his left and walks for 2 Km. He again turns left and walks for 3 Km. At this point he turns to his left and walks for 3 Km. How many kilometers is he from the starting point?
   (a) 1 Km (b) 2 Km
   (c) 3 Km (d) 5 Km

6. A girl leaves from her home. She first walks 30 m in North-West direction and then 30 m in South-West direction. Next, she walks 30 m in South-East direction. Finally, she turns towards her house. In which direction is she moving?
   (a) North-East (b) North-West
   (c) South-East (d) South-West

7. Radha moves towards South-East, a distance of 7 m, then she moves towards West and travels a distance of 14 m. From here, she moves towards North-West a distance of 7 m and finally she moves a distance of 4 m towards East and stands at that point. How far is the starting point from where she now stands?
   (a) 3 m (b) 4 m
   (c) 10 m (d) 11 m

8. A man is facing North-West. He turns 90° in the clockwise direction and then 135° in the anti-clockwise direction. Which direction is he facing now?
   (a) East (b) West
   (c) North (d) South

9. You go North, turn right, then right again and then finally turn left. In which direction are you now?
   (a) North (b) South
   (c) East (d) West

10. Namita walks 14 m towards West, then turns to her right and walks 14 m and then turns to her left and walks 10 m. Again turning to her left she walks 14 m. What is the shortest distance between her starting point and the present position?
    (a) 10 m (b) 24 m
    (c) 28 m (d) 38 m

11. A man is facing South. He turns 135° in the anti-clockwise direction and then 180° in the clockwise direction. Which directions is he facing now?
    (a) North-East
    (b) North-West
    (c) South-East
    (d) South-West

12. Manick walked 40 m towards North, took a left turn and walked 20 m. He again took a left turn and walked 40 m. How far and in which direction is he from the starting point?
    (a) 20 m East
    (b) 20 m North
    (c) 100 m South
    (d) None of these

13. Going 50 m to the South of her house, Radhika turns left and goes another 20 m. Then, turning to the North, she goes 30 m and then starts walking to her house. In which direction is she walking now?
(a) North-West (b) North
(c) South-East (d) East

14. Laxman went 15 Km to the West from my house, then turned left and walked 20 Km. He then returned East and walked 25 Km and finally, turning left covered 20 Km. How far was he from his house?
(a) 5 Km (b) 10 Km
(c) 40 Km (d) 80 Km

15. Amit walked 30 m towards East, took a right turn and walked 40 m. Then he took a left turn and walked 30 m. In which direction is he now from the starting point?
(a) North-East (b) East
(c) South-East (d) South

16. K is 40 m South-West of L. If M is 40 m South-East of L, then in which is M from K?
(a) East (b) West
(c) North-East (d) South

17. A man walks 2 Km towards North. Then he turns to East and walks 10 Km. After this he turns North and walks 3 Km. Again he turns towards East and walks 2 Km. How far is he from the starting point?
(a) 10 Km (b) 13 Km
(c) 15 Km (d) None of these

18. The length and breadth of a room are 8 m and 6 m respectively. A cat runs along all the four walls and finally along a diagonal order to catch a rat. What is the total distance covered by the cat?
(a) 10 m (b) 14 m
(c) 38 m (d) 48 m

19. Sujata started to walk towards the rising Sun. After covering some distance she turned right then again right and after covering some distance she again turns right. Which direction is she facing?
(a) North (b) South
(c) North-East (d) South-West

20. Some boys are sitting in three rows all facing North such that A is in the middle row. P is just to the right of A but in the same row. Q is just behind P while R is to the North of A. In which direction of R is Q?
(a) South (b) South-West
(c) North-East (d) South-East

21. One morning after sunrise, Vimal started to walk. While walking he met Stephen who was coming from the opposite direction. Vimal saw that Stephen's shadow was towards his right. In which direction was Vimal facing?
(a) East (b) West
(c) South (d) Data inadequate

22. Golu started from his house North. After covering a distance of 8 Km he turned left and covered a distance of 6 Km. What is the shortest distance now from his house?
(a) 10 Km (b) 16 Km
(c) 14 Km (d) 2 Km

23. P started from his house towards West. After walking a distance of 25 m he turned to the right and walked 10 m. He then again turned to the right and walked 15 m. After this he is to turn right and cover 30 m. In which direction should he go?
(a) West (b) South
(c) South-West (d) South-East

24. X started to walk straight towards south. After walking 5 m he turned to the left and walked 3 m. After this he turned to the right and walked 5 m. In which direction X is facing?
(a) North-East
(b) South
(c) North
(d) South-West

25. Hemant in order to go to university started from his house in the east and came to a crossing. The road to the left ends in a theatre, straight ahead is the hospital. In which direction is the university?
(a) North (b) South
(c) East (d) West

Mirror and Water Images

6

Chapter Outline:

- ❒ **Mirror Images**
- ❒ **Water Images**
- ❒ **Multiple Choice Questions**

Mirror Images

The image of an object, as seen in a mirror, is called its mirror reflection or mirror image. Mirror image is also known as horizontal plane.

Mirror Images of Capital letters

Letter	Mirror Image	Letter	Mirror Image	Letter	Mirror Image
A	A	J	Ⴑ	S	Ƨ
B	ᗺ	K	ꓘ	T	T
C	Ɔ	L	⅃	U	U
D	ᗡ	M	M	V	V
E	Ǝ	N	И	W	W
F	ꟻ	O	O	X	X
G	Ꭾ	P	ꟼ	Y	Y
H	H	Q	Ϙ	Z	ꙁ
I	I	R	Я	-	-

Mirror Images of Small letters

Letter	Mirror Image	Letter	Mirror Image	Letter	Mirror Image
a	ɒ	j	ᒑ	s	ƨ
b	d	k	ʞ	t	ƚ
c	ɔ	l	l	u	u
d	b	m	m	v	v
e	ɘ	n	n	w	w
f	ᖷ	o	o	x	x
g	ϱ	p	q	y	γ
h	ᖹ	q	p	z	ꙁ
l	l	r	ɿ	-	-

Mirror Images of Numbers

Letter	Mirror Image	Letter	Mirror Image	Letter	Mirror Image
1	Ɩ	4	ᔭ	7	Ɫ
2	Ƨ	5	ट	8	8
3	Ɛ	6	ə	9	ɘ

Water Images

The reflection of an object, as seen in the water, is called its water image. It is the inverted image obtained by turning the object upside down.

Water Images of Capital Letters

Letter	Water Image	Letter	Water Image	Letter	Water Image
A	∀	J	ſ	S	Ƨ
B	B	K	K	T	⊥
C	C	L	Γ	U	∩
D	D	M	W	V	Λ
E	E	N	И	W	M
F	Ⅎ	O	O	X	X
G	⅁	P	b	Y	⅄
H	H	Q	Ò	Z	ꙁ
I	I	R	ᴚ	-	-

Water Images of Small letters

Letter	Water Image	Letter	Water Image	Letter	Water Image
a	ɐ	j	ɾ	s	ƨ
b	p	k	ʞ	t	ʇ
c	c	l	l	u	n
d	q	m	ɯ	v	ʌ
e	ə	n	u	w	ʍ
f	ɟ	o	o	x	x
g	ƃ	p	b	y	ʎ
h	ɥ	q	d	z	ꙁ
l	l	r	ɹ	-	-

Water Images of Numbers

Letter	Water Image	Letter	Water Image	Letter	Water Image
1	⇂	4	ᔭ	7	ㄥ
2	ᘔ	5	ƹ	8	8
3	Ɛ	6	ɘ	9	ə

Multiple Choice Questions

Direction: In each of the following questions you are given a combination of letters and/or numbers followed by four alternatives (1), (2), (3) and (4). Choose the alternative which closely resembles the mirror image of the given combination.

1. 247596

   (1) 695742　　(2) ƧᔭΓƼ69
   (3) ƧᔭΓƼ99　　(4) ƧᔭΓƼ96

   (a) 1　　(b) 2
   (c) 3　　(d) 4

2. BR4AQ16HI

   (1) IHƏ1QAᔭЯ8　　(2) IH61QAᔭЯ8
   (3) IHƏ1QAᔭЯ8　　(4) IH91QAᔭЯ8

   (a) 1　　(b) 2
   (c) 3　　(d) 4

3. GEOGRAPHY

   (1) YHꟼAЯӘOƎӘ　　(2) YHPARGOEG
   (3) ⅄HꟼAЯӘOƎӘ　　(4) YHꟼVЯӘOƎӘ

   (a) 1　　(b) 2
   (c) 3　　(d) 4

4. NATIONAL

   (1) JAИOI⅃AИ　　(2) JAИOITAИ
   (3) JANOITAИ　　(4) LAИOITAИ

   (a) 1　　(b) 2
   (c) 3　　(d) 4

5. PAINTED

   (1) DƎTNIAꟼ　　(2) ᗡƎTNIAꟼ
   (3) DƎ⊥NIAꟼ　　(4) DETИIAꟼ

   (a) 1　　(b) 2
   (c) 3　　(d) 4

6. Choose the correct mirror image of the given figure (X) from amongst the four alternatives.

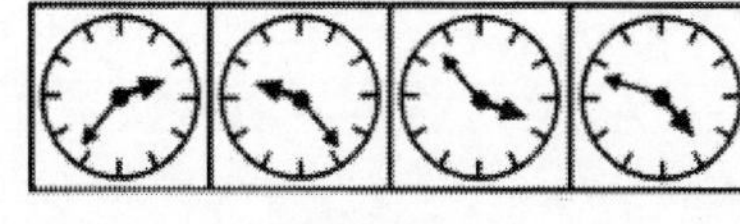

(X)　(1)　(2)　(3)　(4)

(a) 1　　(b) 2
(c) 3　　(d) 4

7. Choose the correct mirror image of the given figure (X) from amongst the four alternatives.

(X)　(1)　(2)　(3)　(4)

(a) 1　　(b) 2
(c) 3　　(d) 4

8. Choose the correct mirror image of the given figure (X) from amongst the four alternatives.

(X)　(1)　(2)　(3)　(4)

(a) 1　　(b) 2
(c) 3　　(d) 4

9. Choose the correct mirror image of the given figure (X) from amongst the four alternatives.

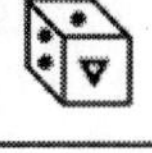

(X)　(1)　(2)　(3)　(4)

(a) 1　　(b) 2
(c) 3　　(d) 4

10. Choose the correct mirror image of the given figure (X) from amongst the four alternatives.

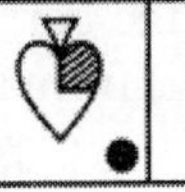
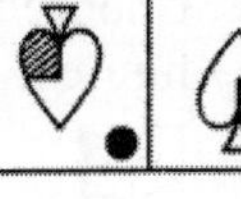

(X)　(1)　(2)　(3)　(4)

(a) 1　　(b) 2
(c) 3　　(d) 4

11. Choose the correct mirror image of the given figure (X) from amongst the four alternatives.

(X)　(1)　(2)　(3)　(4)

(a) 1　　(b) 2
(c) 3　　(d) 4

12. Choose the correct mirror image of the given figure (X) from amongst the four alternatives.

(X) (1) (2) (3) (4)

(a) 1 (b) 2
(c) 3 (d) 4

13. Choose the correct water image of the given figure (X) from amongst the four alternatives.

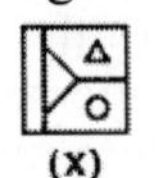
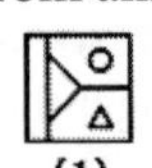

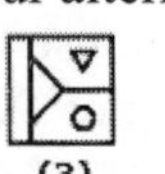
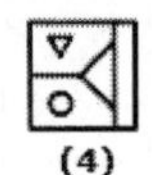

(X) (1) (2) (3) (4)

(a) 1 (b) 2
(c) 3 (d) 4

14. Choose the correct water image of the given figure (X) from amongst the four alternatives.

(X) (1) (2) (3) (4)

(a) 1 (b) 2
(c) 3 (d) 4

15. Choose the correct water image of the given figure (X) from amongst the four alternatives.

(X) (1) (2) (3) (4)

(a) 1 (b) 2
(c) 3 (d) 4

16. Choose the correct water image of the given figure (X) from amongst the four alternatives.

(X) (1) (2) (3) (4)

(a) 1 (b) 2
(c) 3 (d) 4

17. Choose the correct water image of the given figure (X) from amongst the four alternatives.

(X) (1) (2) (3) (4)

(a) 1 (b) 2
(c) 3 (d) 4

18. Choose the correct mirror image of the given figure from amongst the four alternatives.

(a) 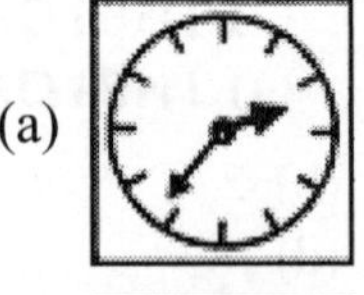 (b) 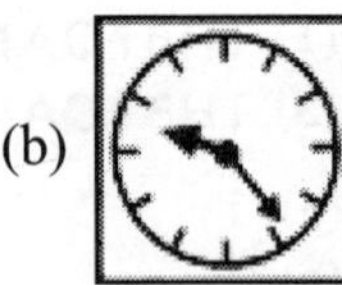

(c) 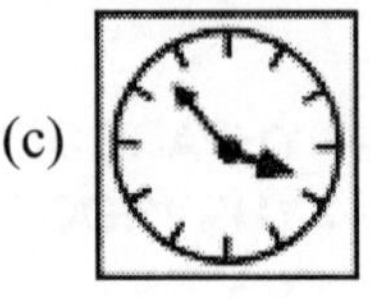 (d) 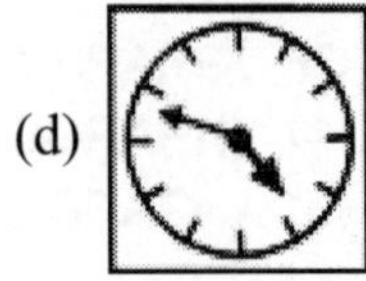

19. Choose the alternative which closely resembles the mirror image of the given combination.

BRISK

(a) ꓘƧIЯᙠ (b) ꓘIƧЯᙠ
(c) ꓘIЯƧᙠ (d) ꓘƧЯIᙠ

20. Choose the alternative which closely resembles the mirror image of the given combination.

123EBDS3FG

(a) ӘꟻƐƧᗡƎᙠƐςƖ
(b) ӘꟻƐƧᗡᙠƎƐςƖ
(c) ӘꟻƐƧᗡƎᙠςƐƖ
(d) ӘƐꟻƧᗡƎᙠςƐƖ

Geometrical Shapes and Solids

7

Chapter Outline:

- ❒ Polygons
- ❒ 2D Shapes
- ❒ 3D Shapes
- ❒ Multiple Choice Questions

We know that lines when joined together form shapes. There are different types of shapes.

Polygons

Shapes that are made of three or more than three lines are called polygons. Each polygon with different number of lines has a different name.

Shown below are different polygons:

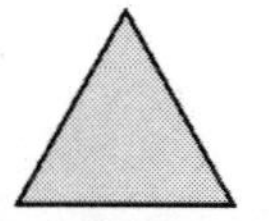
TRIANGLE

SQUARE

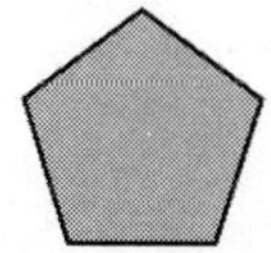
PENTAGON

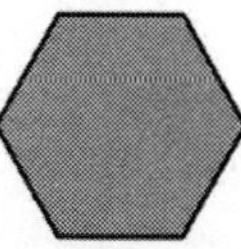
HEXAGON

HEPTAGON

OCTAGON

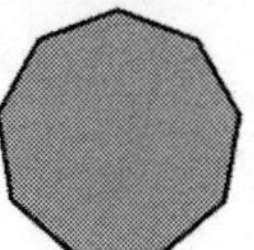
NANOGON

DECAGON

Shapes can also be two dimensional or three dimensional.

2D Shapes

Two dimensional or 2D shapes have length and breath. Some two dimensional shapes are triangle, rectangle, square and circle.

square

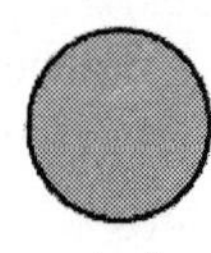
circle

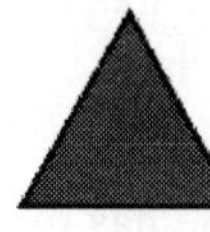
triangle

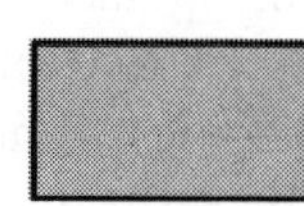
ractangle

3D Shapes

Three dimensional or 3D shapes have length, breadth and thickness. Some three dimensional shapes are cube, cuboid, cone and cylinder.

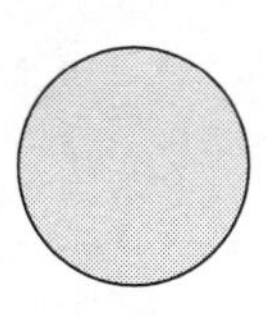
Sphere

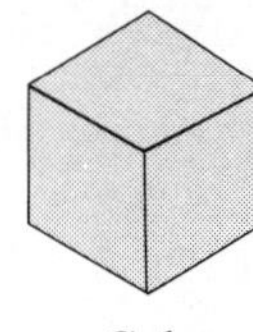
Cube

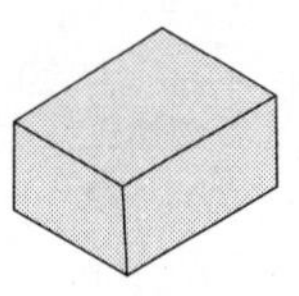
Cuboid

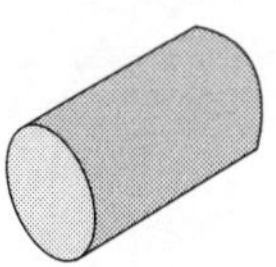
Cylinder

Multiple Choice Questions

1. Which shape has with four equal sides?
   (a) Rectangle (b) Square
   (c) Triangle (d) Heptagon
2. Which shape has three sides?
   (a) Rectangle (b) Square
   (c) Triangle (d) Heptagon
3. Which shape has four sides with only two opposite sides equal?
   (a) Rectangle (b) Square
   (c) Triangle (d) Heptagon
4. Which is a 3D shape?
   (a) Cube (b) Square
   (c) Triangle (d) Hexagon
5. Which is a 2D shape?
   (a) Cube (b) Cuboid
   (c) Sphere (d) Heptagon
6. Which shape has ten sides?
   (a) Rectangle (b) Decagon
   (c) Triangle (d) Heptagon
7. Which shape has nine sides?
   (a) Nanogon (b) Square
   (c) Hexagon (d) Heptagon
8. Which is a polygon?
   (a) Oval (b) Triangle
   (c) Sphere (d) Circle
9. Which is the 3D version of triangle?
   (a) Cone (b) Cube
   (c) Sphere (d) Cuboid
10. Which is 3D version of circle?
    (a) Cone (b) Cube
    (c) Sphere (d) Cuboid
11. Which is the 3D version of square?
    (a) Cone (b) Cube
    (c) Sphere (d) Cuboid
12. Which is the 3D version of rectangle?
    (a) Cone (b) Cube
    (c) Sphere (d) Cuboid
13. What is the shape of a football?
    (a) Cone (b) Cube
    (c) Sphere (d) Cuboid
14. What is the shape of a birthday cap?
    (a) Cone (b) Cube
    (c) Sphere (d) Cuboid
15. What is the shape of a brick?
    (a) Cone (b) Cube
    (c) Sphere (d) Cuboid

Time and Calendar

8

Chapter Outline:

- ❐ Clock and Time
- ❐ Calendar
- ❐ Multiple Choice Questions

Just like you have length to measure your garden, height to measure how tall you are, weight for the mass of your body, time is to measure occurrence of events, events that are happening now or that have happened before.

Just as length, weight or height has units, time also has units. They are years, months, weeks, days, hours, minutes and seconds. To measure hours, minutes and seconds we use a clock.

In a day, we have 24 hours.

Clock and Time

A clock dial has 60 divisions. These divisions show minutes or seconds. There are 12 numerals marked from 1 to 12 on a clock face which are at equal distances.

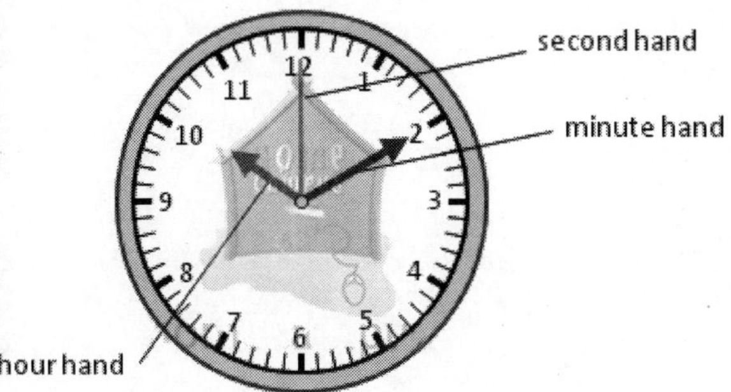

5th division is marked with 1, 10th division with 2 and so are 15th, 20th, 25th, 30th, 35th, 40th, 50th, 55th, and 60th, divisions marked with 3, 4, 5, 6, 7, 8, 9, 10, 11 and 12 respectively. These divisions, generally shown with longer lines than other divisions, represent hours.

The minute hand takes 60 seconds in moving from one division to the next division. This is known as 1 minute.

60 seconds = 1 minute

The minute hand takes 5 minutes to reach from one marked numeral to next marked numeral. And in completing one full revolution it takes 60 minutes. This is called one hour.

60 minutes = 1 hour

An hour hand moves from one numeral to next numeral in 60 minutes.

Further we have the second hand which takes 1 minute to complete one round.

60 seconds = 1 minute

Calendar

There are many ways of measuring time in months, weeks or days and it can be done using a calendar. We have 12 months namely January, February, March, April, May, June, July, August, September, October, November, December. Some months have 30 days and some have 31 days. February is a month in which we have 28 days but every leap year we have February with 29 days.

Further 7 days makes a week.

Names of the days are - Sunday, Monday, Tuesday, Wednesday, Thursday, Friday, Saturday.

Following is the calendar of December 2014:

December 2014

Sunday	Monday	Tuesday	Wednesday	Thursday	Friday	Saturday
	1	2	3	4	5	6
7	8	9	10	11	12	13
14	15	16	17	18	19	20
21	22	23	24	25	26	27
28	29	30	31			

We read the calendar to tell the days and dates. For example, from the above we can see 14th December falls on Sunday.

A date is written as follows:

Date/month/year, example: 14/12/2014

OR

Date-month-year, example: 14-12-2014

OR

Date month, year, example: 14th December 2014.

Multiple Choice Questions

1. Aditya spent 25 minutes on his homework last night. He started it at 5:50 pm. At what time did he finish his homework?
   (a) 5:15 (b) 6:15
   (c) 5:10 (d) 6:10
2. The cricket match started at 8:00 pm. Each half was 45 minutes. At what time did the first half end?
   (a) 8:45 pm
   (b) 9:30 pm
   (c) 8:35 pm
   (d) 9:05 pm
3. The school holiday starts in three weeks. School is open 5 days a week. How many school days are left until the holiday?
   (a) 25 days (b) 21 days
   (c) 15 days (d) 20 days
4. It takes 12 minutes to bathe a dog. How long would it take to bathe 10 dogs?
   (a) 100 minutes
   (b) 3 Hrs
   (c) 60 minutes
   (d) 120 minutes
5. Maheshwari started her homework at 1.25 pm and finished at 2.10 pm. How long did she take to fiish her homework?
   (a) 40 minutes (b) 45 min
   (c) 50 min (d) 55 min
6. Find the odd one out.
   (a) January
   (b) July
   (c) May
   (d) November
7. 00:01: First minute of the day : ______: Last minute of the day.
   (a) 12:59 (b) 24:59
   (c) 23:59 (d) 24:00
8. Ali took 54 minutes to walk to school. His brother took 18 minutes less to walk to the same school. How long did it take Ali's brother to walk to school?
   (a) 30 min (b) 36 min
   (c) 38 min (d) 35 min
9. The Khurana family is going to watch a movie at 5:50 pm. It is 11:20 am right now. How long do they have to wait to watch the movie?
   (a) 5 hours 20 minutes
   (b) 6 and a half hours
   (c) 6 hours
   (d) 6 hours 20 minutes
10. Ayushi slept from 9:00 pm until 7:00 am. She had a bad dream and could not sleep from 2:45 am until 3:30 am. How many hours did she sleep?
    (a) 10 and half hours
    (b) 11 hours 45 minutes
    (c) 9 hours 15 minutes
    (d) 9 hours 45 minutes
11. What does AM stands for?
    (a) After noon
    (b) Before noon
    (c) Midnight
    (d) None of these
12. When do you wish your parents good night?
    (a) AM
    (b) PM
    (c) Evening
    (d) None of these
13. Tina and Mina are traveling to New York City. Tina's plane arrives at 8:00 am. Mina's plane arrives 2 hours and 30 minutes later. What time does Mina's plane arrive?
    (a) 8:30 am (b) 9:30 am
    (c) 10:30 am (d) 11:30 am
14. Today is Monday. After 61 days, it will be
    (a) Wednesday
    (b) Saturday
    (c) Tuesday
    (d) Thursday
15. The difference between 7 hours 25 minutes and 3 hours 45 minutes is
    (a) 4 hrs 15 min
    (b) 4 hrs 65 min
    (c) 3 hrs 40 min
    (d) 4 hrs 45 min

16. The time from 12 midnight to 12 noon is noted as
(a) am (b) pm
(c) midnight (d) day

17. PM means
(a) post meridian
(b) post noon
(c) pre noon
(d) none of these

18. 3 hrs 33 min = ______ min.
(a) 333 (b) 210
(c) 213 (d) 180

19. How many weeks are there in 1 year?
(a) 55 (b) 53
(c) 51 (d) 52

20. The month with neither 31 days nor 30 days is
(a) February (b) April
(c) November (d) December

SECTION 3
ACHIEVERS' SECTION

Higher Order Thinking Skills (HOTS)

1. Computer can perform different types of tasks with the same ease. At one moment, you can use the computer to prepare a letter document and in the next moment you can play music or print a document. What is this characteristic of a computer called?
   (a) Accuracy
   (b) Diligence
   (c) Versatility
   (d) Storage capability
2. Microsoft has announced free windows – Eyes screen reader software that can run on MS-Office 2010, office 2013 and office 365 subscription. What does this software actually do?
   (a) It can be used to verbalize or speak everything on the screen aloud including text, menu, control buttons and other commands.
   (b) It can be used to customize video output.
   (c) It can be used to scan everything on the screen with a blink of an eye.
   (d) All of these
3. Which of the following Indian companies are front runners in cloud adoption and are deriving business value from cloud?
   (a) Zovi
   (b) Narayana Hrudayalaya
   (c) Maharashtra Government
   (d) All of these
4. Identify the following:
   - It is an American software company that provides cloud and virtualization software and services.
   - It has announced to team up with Google to modernize desktops for the mobile cloud Era by providing business with secure, cloud access to windows applications, data and desktops on Google.

   (a) V Mware (b) Hexaware
   (c) TMware (d) Wcloud
5. Match the following.

Column-I	Column-II
(p) Alt + Space bar	(i) Turns full page view on or off
(q) F11	(ii) Opens title bar menu
(r) + B	(iii) Opens windows Mobility Center
(s) + X	(iv) Highlights the first item in System Tray

   (a) (p)–(ii), (q)–(i), (r)–(iv), (s)–(iii)
   (b) (p)–(i), (q)–(iii), (r)–(ii), (s)–(iv)
   (c) (p)–(iii), (q)–(ii), (r)–(i), (s)–(iv)
   (d) (p)–(iv), (q)–(iii), (r)–(ii), (s)–(i)
6. What is the function of keyboard shortcut -

in windows 7?
   (a) Opens the 2nd position pinned application on the taskbar.
   (b) Minimizes all the open windows.
   (c) Opens the 2nd position icon on system tray.
   (d) Opens the start menu.
7. Which of the following steps is correct if you want to insert these stars and banners in your document in MS Word 2010?

   (a) Home tab → Stars group → Shapes
   (b) Home tab → Illustrations group → Stars
   (c) Insert tab → Illustrations group → Stars
   (d) Insert tab → Illustrations group → Shapes

8. Which of the following options is correct regarding the given icon of MS Word 2010?

(a) It colors the background behind the selected text or paragraph.
(b) It comes under paragraph group of Home tab.
(c) You can customize the colors according to your wish.
(d) All of these

9. How can you add colors in the unfilled box in the colors group of Home tab in MS Paint of Windows 7?

(a) Click on <Color 1> button → select Custom Colors in Edit Colors in Edit Colors dialog box → click on 'Add to Custom Colors' → click ok.
(b) Click on <Color 2> button box → select Custom Colors in Edit color dialog box → click on 'Add to Custom Colors' → click ok.
(c) Click on <Edit colors> box → select Custom Color in Edit Color dialog box → click on ' Add To Custom Colors' → click ok.
(d) Both (a) and (b)

10. Find the odd one out.

(a) (b) 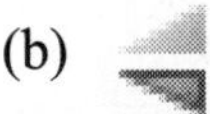

(c) (d) 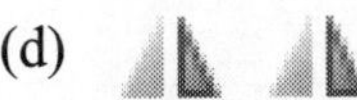

11. ______ was an improved model of IBM – 700 series machines. More than 1000 units were sold for use in business and scientific applications. It was developed in the approximate period of 1953.
(a) IBM-703
(b) IBM-650
(c) IBM-643
(d) IBM-200

12. Which of the following statements is incorrect about second generation computers?
(a) They were manufactured using transistors.
(b) They were more than ten times faster than first generation com-puters.
(c) They were less prone to hardware failures than first generation com-puters.
(d) In these computers, thousands of individual IC chips had to be assembled manually into electronic circuits.

13. Which of the following helps the computer to send only the results for output to an output device and not the intermediate results?
(a) ALU
(b) CU
(c) MU
(d) None of these

14. Some common features of a software package are given below. Identify the software.
- It enables users to draw designs.
- It enables users to create graph and charts.
- It enables users to create their overall designs and pictures much faster by allowing them to use not only the graphic objects or images supplied with software, but even those that are stored in files created by some other software or means.

(a) Graphics Package Software
(b) Personal Assistance Software
(c) Spreadsheet Package
(d) Office Package

15. Which of the following translates a name like shraddhasingh.com into numbers like 16.01.88.04?
(a) DNS
(b) IP address
(c) E-mail
(d) Port

16. www.pinki.info, www.sheetal.net, www.shraddha.name are examples of ______.
(a) Country Domains
(b) Generic Domains
(c) Specialized Domains
(d) Vanity Domains

17. Net 2 phone is a/an ______.
    (a) Internal phone program that allows you to make calls over the internet
    (b) Instant messaging program
    (c) Web editing program
    (d) Tool for participating in newsgroup over telephone
18. Port number for outgoing e-mail is _____ and port number for incoming e-mail is _____.
    (a) 110, 25
    (b) 25, 110
    (c) 80, 25
    (d) 25, 80
19. Which of the following statements is incorrect about screen image projector?
    (a) It projects information from a computer on to a large screen.
    (b) It has become a common presentation equipment today.
    (c) It is an input device.
    (d) None of these.
20. Which of the following windows helps you to browse in stealth mode?
    (a) Incognito mode offered by Google Chrome
    (b) Incognito mode offered by Mozilla
    (c) Incognito mode offered by Internet Explorer
    (d) All of these

Short Answer Questions

1. **What is a Home tab in MS Paint?**

   For nearly everything you do, you will want the Home tab to be at the front. The Home tab contains the Ribbon, from which tools and colors are selected. When you are making use of the View tab, you can flick back and forth between Home and View as often as you need to.

2. **What is the use of Bookmarks/Favorites in web browsers?**

   All major web browsers helps you store links to sites you wish to return to or visit later. Netscape, Mozilla, and Firefox use the term Bookmarks. The equivalent in Internet Explorer (IE) is called a "Favorite." To create a bookmark, click on BOOKMARKS or FAVORITES, then ADD. To visit a bookmarked site, click on BOOKMARKS and select the site from the list.

3. **Define FTP.**

   FTP stands for File Transfer Protocol. It is the ability to quickly transfer entire files from one computer to another, intact for viewing or other purposes.

4. **What is an IP Address?**

   It is a unique number consisting of 4 parts separated by dots, e.g. 155.112.245.4. Every machine that is on the Internet has a unique IP address. If a machine does not have an IP number, it is not really on the Internet.

5. **What is TCP/IP protocol?**

   This is the suite of protocols that defines the Internet. Originally designed for the UNIX operating system, TCP/IP software is now available for every major kind of computer operating system. To be truly on the Internet, your computer must have TCP/IP software.

6. **For what purpose do we use Zoom control?**

   Zoom control lets you zoom in for a closer look at your text. The zoom control consists of a slider that you can slide left or right to zoom in or out. It also has + and – buttons that you can click to increase or decrease the zoom factor.

7. **Define computer network.**

   A group of two or more computer systems together is called a computer network. A good example can be your computer lab.

8. **Differentiate between Internet, Intranet and Extranet.**

Internet	Intranet	Extranet
This is the world wide network of computers accessible to anyone who knows their IP address.	This is a network that is not available to the world outside. It is restricted to a particular area, organization or building.	This is an intranet that is partially accessible to authorized outsiders.

9. **What is Abacus? When was it invented?**

   Invented by Chinese in 16th century, it is the first calculating device used for addition and subtraction.

10. **Write a short note on Napier's Bones.**

    John Napier invented Napier's Bones in which the rods were made of bones with numbers on it and it was used for multiplication and division.

11. **Who invented the Leibnitz calculator?**

    Invented by Gottfried Wilhelm Leibnitz, Leibnitz calculator was the first calculator to perform all four arithmetical operations – addition, subtraction, multiplication and division.

12. **What are different selection options in MS Paint?**

    Crop: The top button, a diamond shape with a line through it, lets you crop your picture so that only the selected area remains.

Resize and Skew: The second tiny button to the right of the large Select button opens the Resize and Skew dialogue box.

Rotate or Flip: This menu lets you make mirror images of selections, either vertically or horizontally, and it also lets you rotate an item 90 degrees.

13. What is HTML? Explain in brief.

HTML Stands for Hypertext Markup Language. HTML is a standardized language of computer code, imbedded in "source" documents behind all web documents, containing the textual content, images, links to other documents, etc.

14. Define Internet and Intranet.

Internet is the vast collection of interconnected networks that use the TCP/IP protocol evolved from the ARPANET of the late 60s and 70s. An "internet" (lower case i) is any computers connected to each other (a network), and are not part of the Internet unless they use TCP/IP protocols. An "intranet" is a private network inside a company or organization that uses the same kinds of software that you would find on the public Internet, but that is only for internal use.

15. What are the two different types of Rulers in MS Word 2010?

Word has two rulers - a horizontal ruler and a vertical ruler. The horizontal ruler appears just beneath the Ribbon and is used to set margins and tab stops. The vertical ruler appears on the left edge of the MS Word window and is used to set the vertical position of elements on the page.

Model Test Paper – 1

Mental Ability

1. What number is shown here?

(a) 90010 (b) 9010
(c) 9000 (d) 9100

2. Farah wants to measure the amount of water this pitcher can hold. Which of the following units of measurement should she use?

(a) Liter
(b) Meter
(c) Kilogram
(d) Centimeter

3. The adjoining chart shows the number of markers in the desks of some students. Which two students have a total number of markers that could be shared equally among three students?

Student	Number of Markers
Sanjay	12
Harsh	19
Naitik	13
Tarun	9

(a) Naitik and Harsh
(b) Naitik and Tarun
(c) Sanjay and Naitik
(d) Sanjay and Tarun

4. Gautam had 40 marbles. He divided the marbles equally among 8 students by putting the marbles in the bags. Which of the following models shows how the 40 marbles were divided?

(a) 

(b) 

(c) 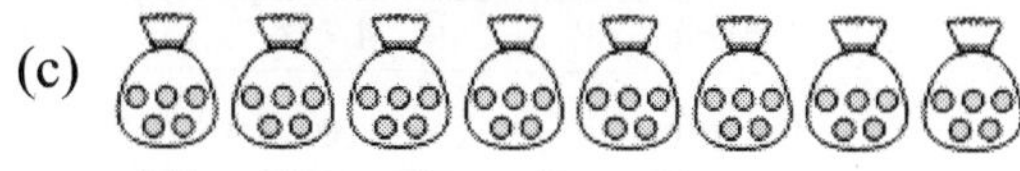

(d) 

5. Look at these numbers.

6 7 8 11

Choose two numbers from the list to complete the multiplication sentence.

$\square \times \square = 88$

(a) 6 and 8
(b) 7 and 8
(c) 8 and 11
(d) 6 and 11

6. Find in the missing number.

$$\begin{array}{r} 947 \\ \times\ 10 \\ \hline 9470 \\ +\ \square \\ \hline 9470 \end{array}$$

(a) 0000 (b) 1111
(c) 1000 (d) 0001

7. Rima added eight thousand, nine hundred and nine. Which number will she get?

(a) 8,904 (b) 8,709
(c) 8,909 (d) 8,919

8. A teacher handed out textbooks for Maths, Hindi, English, Science and Social Studies. There were 22 students in the class. Each student received 1 textbook for each of these subjects. What is the total number of textbooks the teacher handed out?
   (a) 101 (b) 115
   (c) 110 (d) 100

9. Dev read so many number of pages each month as given in the table. In which month did Dev read the most pages?

Pages read	
Month	**Number of Pages**
January	4,176
February	4,416
March	4,768
April	4,716

   (a) January (b) February
   (c) March (d) April

10. What fraction of the figure is unshaded?

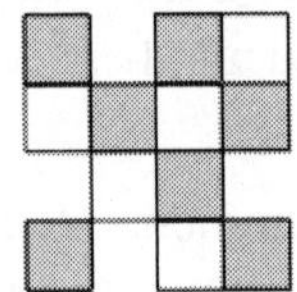

   (a) 7/16 (b) 5/16
   (c) 7/12 (d) 5/12

11. Look at the adjoining group of numbers.

275		481
	103	
367		185

   What do these numbers have in common?
   (a) They are all even numbers less than 500.
   (b) They are all even numbers greater than 200.
   (c) They are all odd numbers less than 500.
   (d) They are all odd numbers greater than 200.

12. Which shape shows the fraction 2/4 shaded?

   (a) 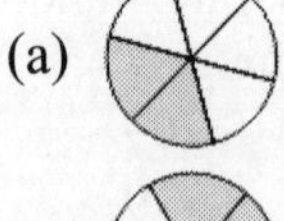 (b) 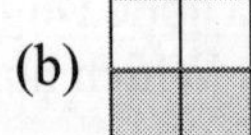

   (c)  (d) 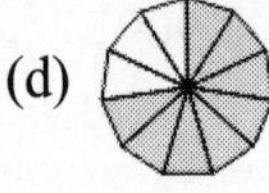

13. Which sign belongs in the blank?
   18 – 1 ___ 3 + (6 + 6)
   (a) <
   (b) =
   (c) >
   (d) Cannot be determined

14. Look at the given pictograph.

	Class reading
June	
July	
August	
September	
October	
November	
Each	= 10 Books

   How many books did the class read in all?
   (a) 220 (b) 22
   (c) 240 (d) 280

15. Akshat saw a shape with 4 sides, with opposite sides parallel. Which shape could Akshat have seen?
   (a) (b)
   (c) (d)

Logical and Analytical Reasoning

16. Vineet put 70 plastic cups in the first stack, 80 plastic cups in the second stack, and 90 plastic cups in the third stack. If this pattern continues, how many plastic cups will Vineet put in the fourth stack?
   (a) 100 (b) 108
   (c) 106 (d) 107

17. I am a two-digit number. I have seven in the ten's place. You say me when you count by ten's. What number am I?
   (a) 77 (b) 70
   (c) 17 (d) 700

18. How much does cost?

   (a) Rs. 5 (b) Rs. 3
   (c) Rs. 4 (d) Rs. 2

19. Nikita drove from her house to the park. She drove 15 blocks East, 10 blocks North, 15 blocks West, 5 blocks North and stopped at the park. Where is the park in relation to Nikita's house?
    (a) 15 blocks North
    (b) 5 blocks North
    (c) 45 blocks West
    (d) 15 blocks East

20. The given table shows the total number of plants Aman has in different rows in his garden. Which of the following correctly describes the relationship in the table?

Aman's Garden	
Number of Rows	**Total Number of Plants**
2	14
4	28
5	35
5	35

    (a) Number of rows ÷ 2 = total number of plants
    (b) Number of rows × 14 = total number of plants
    (c) Number of rows ÷ 7 = total number of plants
    (d) Number of rows × 7 = total number of plants

21. Aryan made a secret code with symbols. All of his symbols shared a common characteristic. Some of the symbols for his code are shown below.

    Γ ⊫ ⊣ ǂ

    These are not part of Aryan's secret code.

    ∥ ⋇ Ʒ ⋦

    Which of the following could be part of Aryan's code?
    (a) ≡   (b) ∨
    (c) ⊥   (d) χ

22. Preeti made the given input-output table. What is the output when the input is 24?

Input	6	18	24	30	36
Output	2	6	?	10	12

    (a) 3   (b) 7
    (c) 8   (d) 9

23. Ishika made bracelets for her friends. The diagram given below shows the choices of bead shapes and colours available.

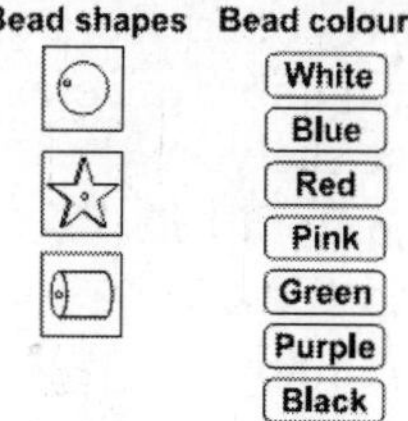

    How many different combinations of 1 bead shape and 1 bead colour are possible?
    (a) 21   (b) 14
    (c) 10   (d) 28

24. Lakshay's number machine follows the same rule each time he puts in a number. Lakshay puts the number 10 into his machine. What number will come out?

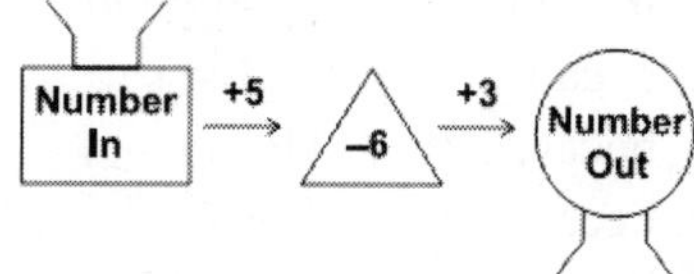

    (a) 20   (b) 15
    (c) 12   (d) 2

25. How many unit cubes (☐) are needed to make the given solid figure?

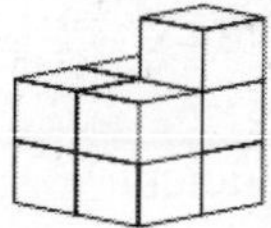

    (a) 5   (b) 7
    (c) 8   (d) 9

26. Look at the given pattern. How would you show this pattern using letters?

    (a) ABA   (b) AAB
    (c) ABC   (d) AB

27. How has this figure been transformed?

    R → ꓤ

    It has been ______.
    (a) Reflected
    (b) Rotated
    (c) Translated
    (d) Shifted

28. At a grocery store, there were 180 cereal boxes on the shelves. There were 6 different brands of cereals, and there were an equal number of boxes of each brand. How can you determine the number of cereal boxes of each brand on these shelves?
(a) Subtract 6 from 180
(b) Add 6 and 180
(c) Multiply 180 by 6
(d) Divide 180 by 6

29. The list given below shows the number of students out of 30 who choose different foods in the cafeteria.
- 11 students choose pizza.
- 4 students choose burger.
- 3 students choose sandwich.
- ______ students choose salad.

How many students choose salad?
(a) 18, because $11 + 4 + 3 = 18$
(b) 26, because $30 - (11 - 4 - 3) = 26$
(c) 12, because $30 - 11 - 4 - 3 = 12$
(d) 20, because $30 - (11 - 4) - 3 = 20$

30. The vanilla cake is larger than the coconut cake. The vanilla cake is smaller than the chocolate cake. Which cake is the smallest?
(a) Chocolate cake
(b) Coconut cake
(c) Vanilla cake
(d) Data is insuficient

Computers & Information Technology

31. The part of computer that performs all mathematical and logical operations is ______.
(a) CPU (b) Keyboard
(c) Calculator (d) Motherboard

32. Which of the following buttons will you use to multiply two numbers using a computer calculator?
(a) l (b) +
(c) * (d) /

33. , , , 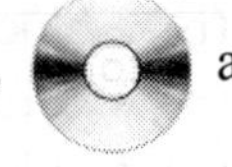 are termed as ______.
(a) Peripherals
(b) Programs
(c) Software
(d) Input devices

34. Match the following.

i. A	1. Fill
ii.	2. Text
iii.	3. Magnifier
iv.	4. Brush

(a) (i) → 2, (ii) → 1, (iii) → 4, (iv) → 3
(b) (i) → 3, (ii) → 2, (iii) → 4, (iv) → 1
(c) (i) → 2, (ii) → 4, (iii) → 3, (iv) → 1
(d) (i) → 4, (ii) → 3, (iii) → 2, (iv) → 1

35. You have a great picture of your new bicycle, that you want to send to your friend. The way to put the picture into the computer is ______.
(a) By scanning it
(b) By printing it
(c) By copying it
(d) By saving it

Model Test Paper – 2

Mental Ability

1. From the digits 2, 5, 8, 7 and 3, form the smallest 5 digit even number and the greatest 5 digit odd number. The difference between the numbers is ______.
   (a) 23578 (b) 63945
   (c) 63954 (d) 87523

2. On adding 254 to the remainder when 542 is divided by 6 gives A. What is A?
   (a) 252 (b) 2
   (c) 256 (d) 260

3. What fraction of the square is shaded?

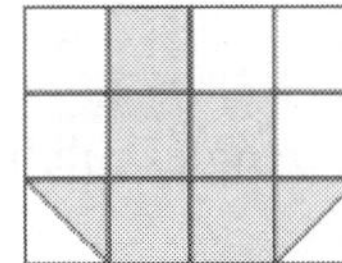

   (a) 1/4 (b) 1/2
   (c) 2/3 (d) 7/12

4. How many numbers between 10 and 30 are multiples of either 5 or 3 including 10 and 30?
   (a) 12 (b) 13
   (c) 15 (d) 10

5. Mona wakes up at 6:15 am. She takes 25 minutes to take bath, 15 minutes to eat breakfast and 20 minutes to walk to school. At what time will she reach school?

   (a) 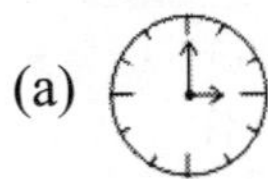 (b) 

   (c) 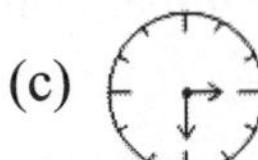 (d) 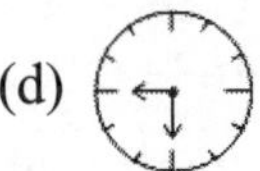

6. Which of the following is not correctly matched?
   (a) 50 → L (b) 500 → D
   (c) 1000 → DLD (d) 100 → C

7. Harsh collected 124 stamps and Harry collected 47 stamps. How many stamps must Harsh give to Harry so that Harry has half of what Harsh has now?
   (a) 8 (b) 10
   (c) 12 (d) 15

8. Normal body temperature is 37°C. When Rita was ill, her temperature rose by 2°C. What was her temperature when she was ill?
   (a) 39°C (b) 40°C
   (c) 42°C (d) 45°C

9. What is the weight of one cone?

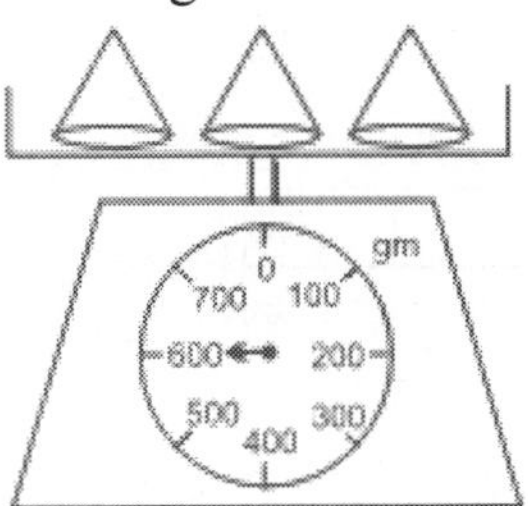

   (a) 220 gm (b) 250 gm
   (c) 350 gm (d) 200 gm

10. Mr. Mohit bought 1300 apples. He threw away 52 rotten apples. He then put the remaining apples equally into 8 boxes. How many apples did he put into each box?
   (a) 150 (b) 156
   (c) 162 (d) 165

11. Lipika gave the cashier a 1000 rupee note for one toy car and two toy motorcycles. How much change did she receive from the cashier?

   (a) ₹ 300 (b) ₹ 500
   (c) ₹ 400 (d) ₹ 450

12. Look at these blocks.

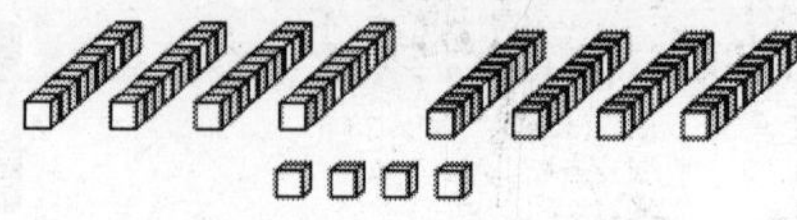

Key
represents 1 block

What number do the blocks represent?

(a) 28 (b) 84
(c) 80 (d) 40

13. In which design do 3/5 of the tiles have pictures of flowers?

(a)

(b) 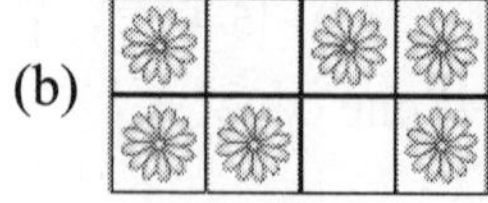

(c) 

(d) 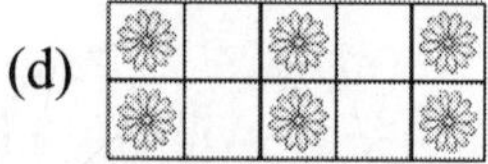

14. Kirti, Misha, Sasha and Annie sold some of their cards at a yard sale. According to the chart, who sold the most cards?

Child	Cards before sale	Cards after sale
Kirti	430	181
Misha	789	671
Sasha	931	688
Annie	842	579

(a) Kirti (b) Misha
(c) Sasha (d) Annie

15. What do these figures have in common?

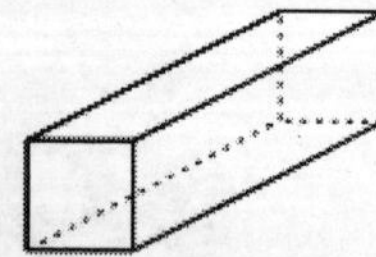 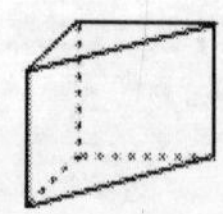

(a) Both have at least one triangular face.
(b) Both have at least one rectangular face.
(c) Both have six faces.
(d) Both have eight vertices.

Logical and Analytical Reasoning

16. Jian made a pattern of numbers with cards.

34	24	14	4

Which rule describes the pattern of numbers on the cards?

(a) Subtract 10
(b) Subtract 14
(c) Multiply by 2
(d) Multiply by 4 17.

17. If □ + □ = ○, ○ + △ = 5 and △ + △ = 6, then □ = ?

(a) 1 (b) 0
(c) 2 (d) 3

18. The given figure is made up of 4 squares.

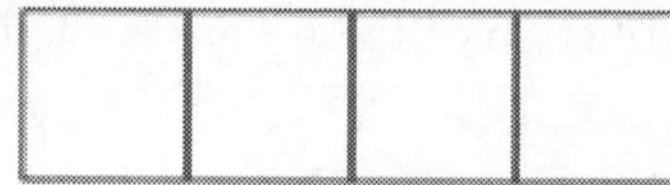

How many rectangles of all sizes are there in the figure?

(a) 6 (b) 3
(c) 5 (d) 4

19. If yesterday was Saturday, what day of the week will it be 7 days from today?

(a) Saturday
(b) Sunday
(c) Monday
(d) Tuesday

20. Find the missing number.

123 [861] 7 [357] 51 [459] 9 [?] 102

(a) 93 (b) 111
(c) 918 (d) 981

21. What are the next three numbers in this pattern?

1,878	1,882	1,886	1,890	1,894

(a) 1,898 | 1,802 | 1,806

(b) 1,898 | 1,902 | 1,906

(c) 1,900 | 1,902 | 1,904

(d) 1,900 | 1,908 | 1,918

22. Which figure will complete the given figure to make a triangle?

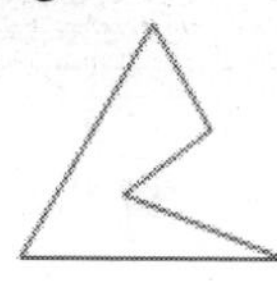

(a)  (b) 

(c) 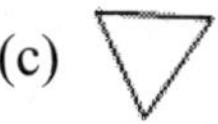 (d) 

23. What is the mirror image of  ?

(a)  (b) 

(c) 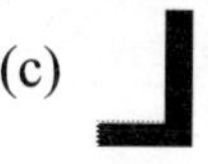 (d) 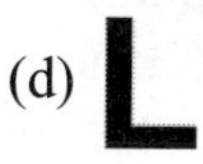

24. In which figure is embedded?

(a)  (b) 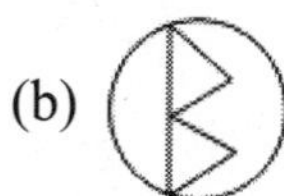

(c) 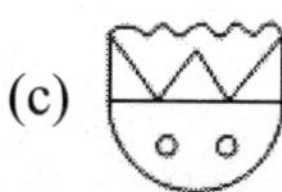 (d) 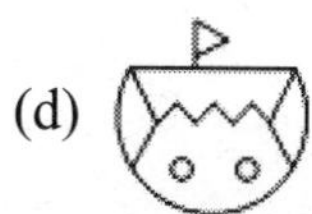

25. Count the number of triangles in the given figure.

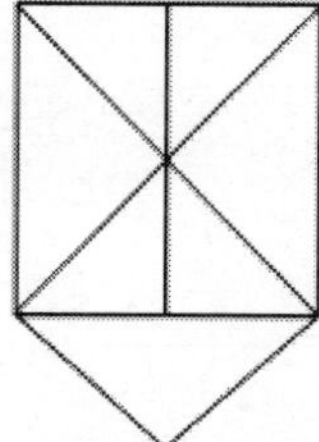

(a) 12 (b) 13
(c) 11 (d) 14

26. Aki made a pattern by putting beads on a string. If the pattern continues in the same way, which bead should be the next?

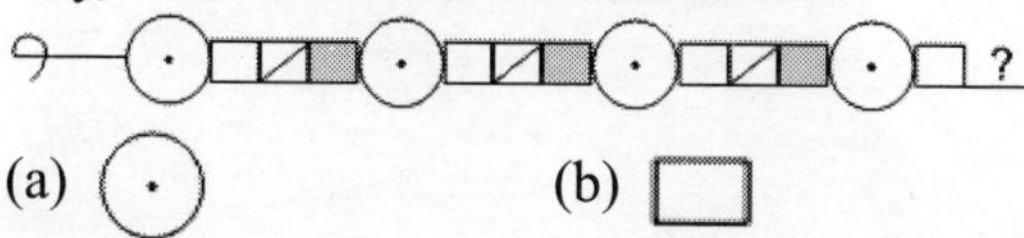

27. If in a certain language "RAM" means "MAR" and "GIRL" means "LRIG" then "WATER" will be coded as ______.
(a) REWAT (b) RETWA
(c) RETAW (d) TAWRE

28. Ali and John like to eat burgers. John and Aman like to eat chips. Ali and Ansh like to eat ice-cream. If burger and ice-cream are served, which child will be the most delighted?
(a) Ali (b) John
(c) Aman (d) Ansh

29. Geetu folded a square piece of paper in half. She then folded the paper in half again. Which of the following cannot be the paper when she unfolds it?

(a) 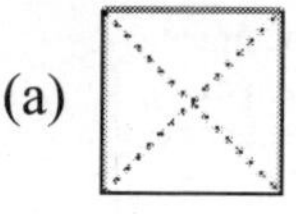 (b) 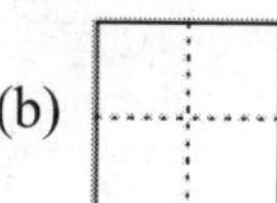

(c) 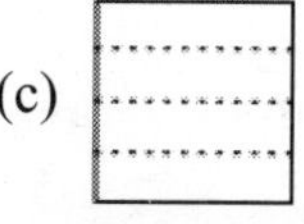 (d) 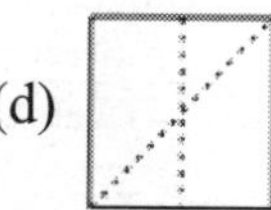

30. The bags shown below contain different kinds of candy bars. Each bag has a different number of candy bars inside.

Nicker Bars

3 candy bars

Choco Bars

5 candy bars

Sesame Bars

2 candy bars

Fruit Bars

4 candy bars

Julie wants to buy 9 candy bars. She can only buy unopened bags of candy. She can buy more than one bag of any type of candy to get her 9 candy bars. Which of the following can be the way in which she can buy candies?
(a) 1 nicker bar bag and 1 choco bar bag
(b) 2 choco bar bag and 2 sesame bar bag
(c) 1 fruit bar bag and 1 choco bar bag
(d) 2 nicker bars bag and 1 fruit bar bag

Computers & Information Technology

31. What general term describes the physical equipment of a computer system, such as its video screen, keyboard and storage devices?
(a) Hardware (b) Input
(c) Software (d) Output

32. Creating an MS Word document would accomplish all of the following tasks except which one?
    (a) Developing a table of historical events
    (b) Calculating the expenditures for the candy sale
    (c) Typing a letter to a friend
    (d) Writing an essay for history class
33. Which key moves the cursor to the beginning of the next line of text?
    (a) Shift (b) Enter
    (c) Tab (d) Backspace
34. You want to change the appearance of a document from that shown in Figure 1 to that shown in Figure 2.

This document will change in appearance deranging on what is selected in pace setup.	This document will change in appearance depending on what is selected in page setup.
Figure 1	Figure 2

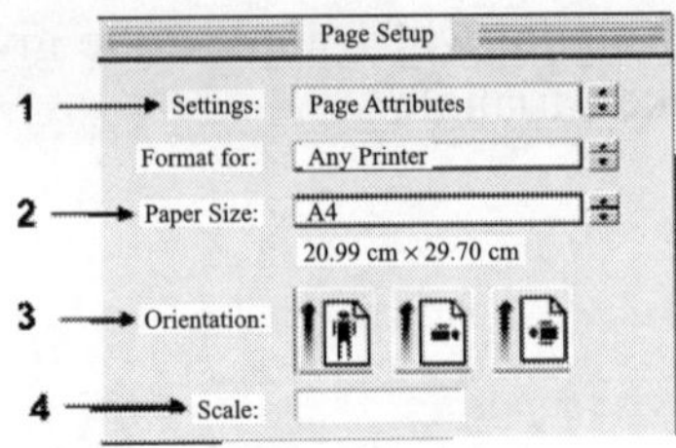

Which area in the Page Setup dialogue box should you select?
    (a) 1 (b) 2
    (c) 3 (d) 4
35. Yesterday, Komal wrote a story using her word processing program. Today, she wants to print the story. What must she do before she can print the story?
    (a) Nothing, just print the story
    (b) Check her handwritten copy
    (c) Save the story
    (d) Retrieve the story

❖❖❖

Hints and Solutions

SECTION 1 : COMPUTERS AND IT

1. FUNDAMENTALS OF COMPUTER

Answer Key									
1. (c)	2. (c)	3. (c)	4. (d)	5. (a)	6. (a)	7. (d)	8. (d)	9. (d)	10. (a)
11. (b)	12. (d)	13. (b)	14. (a)	15. (d)	16. (b)	17. (b)	18. (d)	19. (a)	20. (b)
21. (a)	22. (b)	23. (d)	24. (b)	25. (b)	26. (d)	27. (c)	28. (c)	29. (a)	30. (b)
31. (b)	32. (d)	33. (b)	34. (d)	35. (a)	36. (b)	37. (d)	38. (c)	39. (b)	40. (b)
41. (a)	42. (d)	43. (b)	44. (c)	45. (b)	46. (c)	47. (c)	48. (a)	49. (b)	50. (a)

2. EVOLUTION OF COMPUTER

Answer Key									
1. (b)	2. (c)	3. (d)	4. (c)	5. (a)	6. (d)	7. (b)	8. (b)	9. (b)	10. (b)
11. (a)	12. (b)	13. (a)	14. (a)	15. (a)	16. (a)	17. (a)	18. (d)	19. (b)	20. (b)
21. (d)	22. (b)	23. (b)	24. (d)	25. (b)					

3. MS WORD 2010

Answer Key									
1. (d)	2. (b)	3. (c)	4. (c)	5. (d)	6. (c)	7. (b)	8. (d)	9. (a)	10. (c)
11. (d)	12. (a)	13. (d)	14. (b)	15. (b)	16. (d)	17. (d)	18. (a)	19. (c)	20. (c)
21. (c)	22. (a)	23. (c)	24. (c)	25. (c)					

4. MS PAINT

Answer Key									
1. (c)	2. (b)	3. (b)	4. (c)	5. (c)	6. (c)	7. (a)	8. (b)	9. (a)	10. (c)
11. (c)	12. (b)	13. (d)	14. (d)	15. (a)	16. (d)	17. (a)	18. (d)	19. (a)	20. (d)

5. NETWORK

Answer Key									
1. (a)	2. (c)	3. (d)	4. (c)	5. (a)	6. (a)	7. (b)	8. (d)	9. (b)	10. (a)
11. (b)	12. (a)	13. (b)	14. (a)	15. (b)	16. (a)	17. (d)	18. (b)	19. (a)	20. (a)

6. INTERNET AND ITS USES

Answer Key									
1. (b)	2. (d)	3. (a)	4. (a)	5. (d)	6. (c)	7. (b)	8. (c)	9. (b)	10. (d)
11. (a)	12. (a)	13. (b)	14. (d)	15. (d)	16. (b)	17. (a)	18. (b)	19. (a)	20. (d)
21. (b)	22. (d)	23. (d)	24. (b)	25. (b)					

7. WINDOWS 7

Answer Key									
1. (b)	2. (b)	3. (c)	4. (b)	5. (d)	6. (c)	7. (d)	8. (c)	9. (d)	10. (d)
11. (a)	12. (d)	13. (d)	14. (c)	15. (b)	16. (c)	17. (a)	18. (b)	19. (b)	20. (a)

8. LATEST DEVELOPMENTS IN IT

Answer Key									
1. (d)	2. (c)	3. (b)	4. (a)	5. (b)	6. (b)	7. (d)	8. (d)	9. (b)	10. (c)
11. (d)	12. (b)	13. (c)	14. (c)	15. (a)	16. (c)	17. (d)	18. (c)	19. (c)	20. (d)
21. (b)	22. (a)	23. (a)	24. (b)	25. (d)					

SECTION 2 : LOGICAL REASONING

1. PATTERNS

Answer Key									
1. (d)	2. (c)	3. (d)	4. (a)	5. (c)	6. (d)	7. (c)	8. (d)	9. (b)	10. (d)
11. (a)	12. (d)	13. (d)	14. (a)	15. (b)	16. (b)	17. (c)	18. (a)	19. (b)	20. (c)
21. (a)	22. (c)	23. (d)	24. (b)	25. (a)	26. (d)	27. (b)	28. (a)	29. (c)	30. (d)
31. (b)	32. (a)	33. (c)	34. (d)	35. (d)	36. (b)	37. (a)	38. (c)	39. (b)	40. (b)
41. (c)	42. (b)	43. (d)	44. (a)	45. (c)	46. (b)	47. (c)	48. (a)	49. (d)	50. (c)

1. **(d)** D + 1 = E, G + 1 = H, L + 1 = M but O – 1 = N.
3. **(d)** R – 1 = Q, N – 1 = M, J – 1 = I but P + 1 = Q.
4. **(a)** V + 1 = W, S + 1 = T, P + 1 = Q but X + 2 = Z.
5. **(c)** Pattern is reverse writing of letters. Z ← Y ← X; W ← V ← U; T ← S ← R but it is not so in case of LMC.
6. **(d)** Pattern is writing continuous three digits. 2 → 3 → 4; 3 → 4 → 5; 4 → 5 → 6 but it is not so in case of D.
10. **(d)** Except for option (d), rest are all are palindrome numbers. Palindrome are the numbers which are same when read from either side. Example: 12421.
11. **(a)** Roof is not a part of the plant.
12. **(d)** Maths is a subject while other options are stationary items.
13. **(d)** Cycle has only two wheels and moves on pedaling.
14. **(a)** Walk is done by foot unlike other options which are done by transport.
16. **(b)** The answer is G as it completes the first word; BEG and also begins the second word GAS.
17. **(c)** The answer is H as it completes the first word; BOTH and also begins the second word HURT.
18. **(a)** The answer is P as it completes the first word; SHARP and also begins the second word PRINT.
19. **(b)** The answer is L as it completes the first word; CAMEL and also begins the second word LIGHT.
20. **(c)** The answer is D as it completes the first word; HAND and also begins the second word DATE.
23. **(d)** The answer is E as it completes the first word; DUCK and also begins the second word KITE.
25. **(a)** The answer is N as it completes the first word; RUIN and also begins the second word NEAR.
26. **(d)** F + 1 = G; B + 2 = D. Similarly, P + 1 = Q, M + 2 = O.
27. **(b)** N – 2 = L; A + 5 = F. Similarly, X – 2 = V, N + 5 = S.
28. **(a)** F – 2 = D; H – 2 = F. Similarly, U – 2 = S, Y – 2 = W.
30. **(d)** D + 1 = E; I – 4 = E. Similarly, R + 1 = S, Q – 4 = M.
35. **(d)** F + 4 = J; G + 4 = K. Similarly, N + 4 = R, O + 4 = S.
41. **(c)** X – 1 = W; W – 1 = V; V – 1 = U; U – 1 = T; T – 1 = S.
42. **(b)** W – 1 = V; V – 2 = T; T – 3 = Q; Q – 4 = M; M – 5 = H.
43. **(d)** A + 1 = B; B + 3 = E; E + 5 = J; J + 7 = Q; Q + 9 = Z.
47. **(c)** 4 + 1 = 5; 5 + 2 = 7; 7 + 3 = 10; 10 + 4 = 14; 14 + 5 = 19.
48. **(a)** 27 – 2 = 25; 25 – 3 = 22; 22 – 4 = 18; 18 – 5 = 13; 13 – 6 = 7.

2. ANALOGY AND CLASSIFICATION

Answer Key

1. (c)	2. (c)	3. (b)	4. (c)	5. (a)	6. (d)	7. (b)	8. (c)	9. (b)	10. (c)
11. (b)	12. (c)	13. (b)	14. (c)	15. (d)	16. (c)	17. (b)	18. (d)	19. (c)	20. (b)

1. **(c)** Second denotes the purpose for which the first is used.
2. **(c)** Second contains an account of the first.
3. **(b)** Second is the working place of the first.
4. **(c)** Jade is a green precious stone and garnet is a red precious stone.
5. **(a)** Second is the place for the first to perform on.
6. **(d)** Second denotes the place where the first is kept and reared.
7. **(b)** First denotes the act leaving the post of the second willingly.

8. **(c)** First is used to cut the second.
9. **(b)** Second is the tool used by the first.
10. **(c)** First is a type of second.
11. **(b)** Rouble is the currency of Estonia and Peso is the currency of Chile.
12. **(c)** First tackles the second.
13. **(b)** Tie is worn in the neck and belt is worn on the waist.
14. **(c)** Oriya is the language of Orissa and Dogri is the language of Jammu.
15. **(d)** Satyajit Ray is a famous personality in the field of films. Similarly, Picasso is an eminent painter.

3. CODING AND DECODING

Answer Key

1. (F)	2. (G)	3. (J)	4. (a)	5. (I)	6. (H)	7. (c)	8. (b)	9. (E)	10. (d)
11. (d)	12. (c)	13. (a)	14. (d)	15. (b)	16. (b)	17. (b)	18. (a)	19. (a)	20. (a)

1. **(F)** Observe the table and take the code for each letter. So, the code for JDRU is 'afqr.'
2. **(G)** Observe the table and take the code for each letter. So, the code for CVFO is 'nslb.'
3. **(J)** Observe the table and take the code for each letter. So, the code for MFHB is 'vlib.'
4. **(a)** Observe the table and take the code for each letter. So, the code for JAZH is 'aegi.'
5. **(I)** Observe the table and take the code for each letter. So, the code for QUNT is 'cruo.'
6. **(H)** Observe the table and take the code for each letter. So, the code for WESI is 'tydo.'
7. **(c)** Observe the table and take the code for each letter. So, the code for CDOK is 'nfbk.'
8. **(b)** Observe the table and take the code for each letter. So, the code for MEUX is 'vyrj.'
9. **(E)** Observe the table and take the code for each letter. So, the code for QEOU is 'cybr.'
10. **(d)** Observe the table and take the code for each letter. So, the code for WJSF is 'tadi.'

4. ALPHABET AND RANKING TEST

Answer Key

1. (c)	2. (d)	3. (a)	4. (a)	5. (c)	6. (c)	7. (b)	8. (b)	9. (d)	10. (c)
11. (c)	12. (b)	13. (a)	14. (a)	15. (a)	16. (a)	17. (d)	18. (c)	19. (c)	20. (b)
21. (c)	22. (d)	23. (d)	24. (a)	25. (d)	26. (c)	27. (c)	28. (d)	29. (a)	30. (b)

1. **(c)** R S T U V
   T is exactly between R and V.
2. **(d)** There are 26 letters in the English alphabet. M and N are the two letters in between, but no single letter exists between M and N.
6. **(c)** F + 6 => L + 6 => R + 6 => X
   Options A, B, and D are not at an internal of 6.
7. **(b)** A C E G I K M O Q S U W Y
   There are 13 letters. You can also count like, there are 26 letters in the alphabet and since every alternate letter is deleted, there will be exactly half the letters.
11. **(c)** The letter I occurs twice in INDIA and the same letter repeats twice in BRITAIN.
12. **(b)** There are two letters P and R which repeats twice, but P does not exist in the word OVERTAKE. Hence, R is the answer.
15. **(b)** N is the letter which exists twice in BEGINNER and once in GINGER and the same letter is not in DIVIDE.
18. **(c)** M L K J I H G F E D C B A N O P Q R S T U V W X Y Z
    A is the thirteenth letter.

22. **(d)** The letter E occurs twice in POMEGRANATE and PINEAPPLE but only once in PROPERLY.

23. **(d)** The letters I and T occurs twice in IMITATE and INTENTION but I occurs twice in INTERIOR hence T is the answer which occurs only once.

29. **(a)** I occurs twice in all the three words.

30. **(b)** The letter A occurs in IDEA and is not in the word IDLE but exist in DEAL.

5. DIRECTION SENSE TEST

Answer Key

1. (b)	2. (d)	3. (c)	4. (c)	5. (a)	6. (a)	7. (c)	8. (b)	9. (c)	10. (b)
11. (d)	12. (d)	13. (a)	14. (b)	15. (c)	16. (a)	17. (b)	18. (c)	19. (a)	20. (d)
21. (c)	22. (a)	23. (c)	24. (b)	25. (a)					

4. **(c)** The man firstly faces the direction OA. On moving 45 degree clockwise, he faces the direction OB. Now again he moved 180 degree clockwise, now he will be facing OC. From here he moved 45 degree anticlockwise, Finally he is facing OD, which is South direction.

7. **(c)** Radha's movements are shown as below:

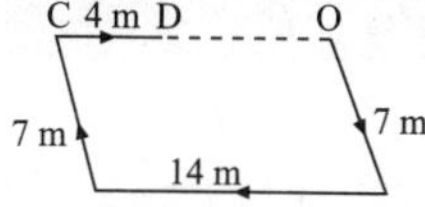

Radha's distance from starting point O = OD
= (OC – CD) = (AB – CD)
= (14 – 4) m = 10 m

10. **(b)** Namita's movements of Namita are as shown in figure (A to B, B to C, C to D and D to E). Clearly, Namita's distance from his initial position

= AE = (AB + BE)
= (AB + CD)
= (14 + 10) m = 24 m.

13. **(a)**

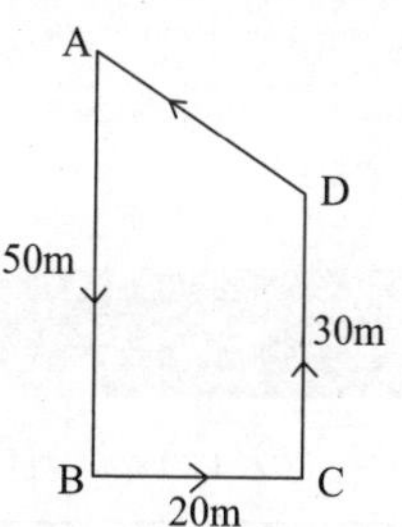

Radhika's movements are as shown in Fig. (A to B, B to C, C to D and D to A).

Clearly, she is finally moving in the direction DA i.e. North

16. **(a)**

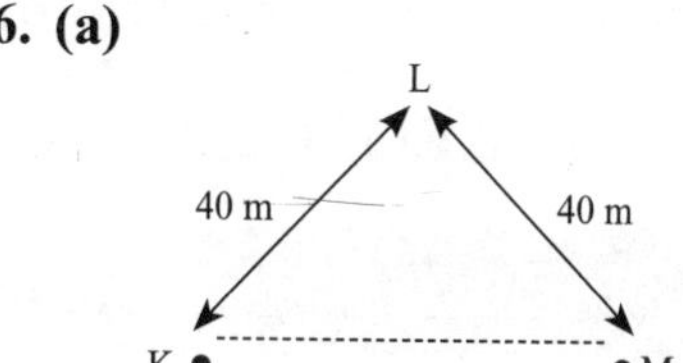

Hence, M is in the East of K

19. **(a)**

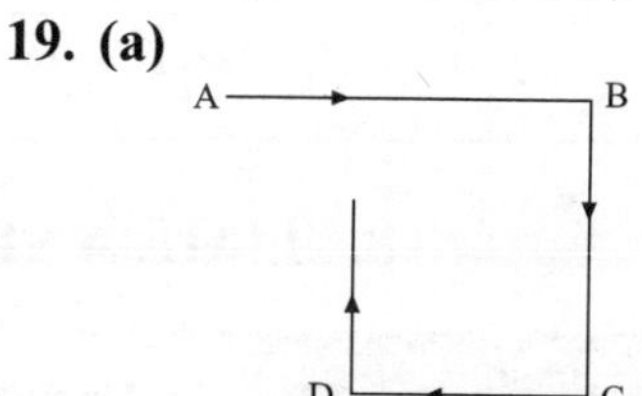

Hence, finally Sujata will face towards North

21. **(c)** Sun rises in the east. So the shadow of a man will always falls towards the west. Since the shadow of Stephen is to the right of Vimal. Hence Vimal is facing towards South.

23. **(c)**

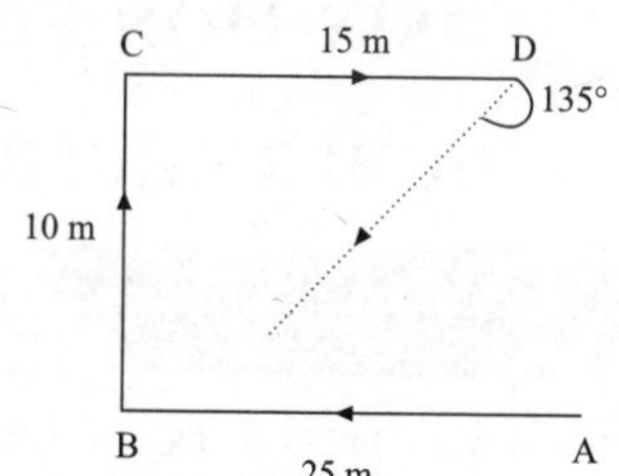

Hence, he should go in the South-West direction.

24. (b)

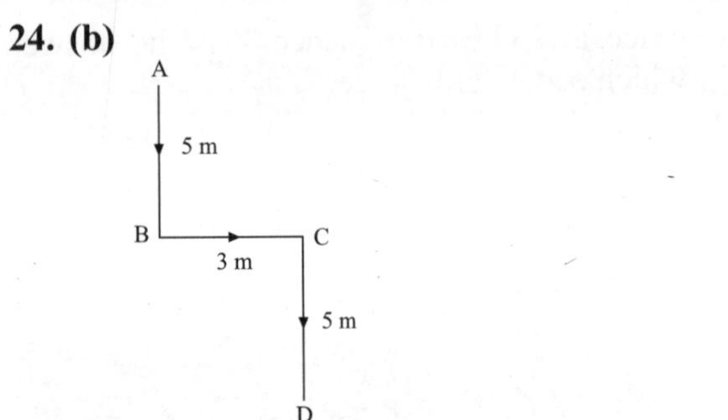

Hence, X will face in the end towards South

25. (a)

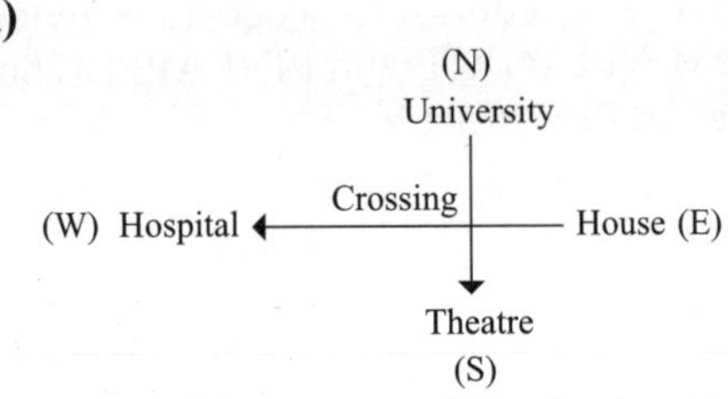

Therefore, university is in North.

6. MIRROR AND WATER IMAGES

Answer Key									
1. (d)	2. (a)	3. (a)	4. (b)	5. (b)	6. (d)	7. (c)	8. (b)	9. (c)	10. (a)
11. (c)	12. (a)	13. (b)	14. (b)	15. (d)	16. (a)	17. (c)	18. (d)	19. (a)	20. (b)

7. GEOMETRICAL SHAPES AND SOLIDS

Answer Key									
1. (b)	2. (c)	3. (a)	4. (a)	5. (d)	6. (b)	7. (a)	8. (b)	9. (a)	10. (c)
11. (b)	12. (d)	13. (c)	14. (a)	15. (d)					

8. TIME AND CALENDAR

Answer Key									
1. (b)	2. (a)	3. (c)	4. (d)	5. (b)	6. (d)	7. (c)	8. (b)	9. (b)	10. (c)
11. (b)	12. (b)	13. (c)	14. (b)	15. (b)	16. (a)	17. (a)	18. (c)	19. (d)	20. (a)

SECTION 3 : ACHIEVERS' SECTION

HIGHER ORDER THINKING SKILLS (HOTS)

Answer Key									
1. (c)	2. (a)	3. (d)	4. (a)	5. (a)	6. (a)	7. (d)	8. (d)	9. (c)	10. (d)
11. (d)	12. (d)	13. (b)	14. (a)	15. (a)	16. (b)	17. (a)	18. (b)	19. (c)	20. (a)

OMR ANSWER SHEET

1. NAME (IN ENGLISH CAPITAL LETTERS ONLY)

2. FATHER'S NAME (IN ENGLISH CAPITAL LETTERS ONLY)

Students must write and darken the respective circles completely for School Code, Class and Roll No. columns, othewise their Answer Sheets will not be evaluated.

3. SCHOOL CODE

A–Z	A–Z	0–9	0–9	0–9	0–9

4. % of Marks / Grade

In Last Class

Percentage OR Grade

0–9	0–9	0–9	A–J

5. CLASS

0, 1, 2	0, 1, 2, 4, 5, 6, 7, 8, 9, M, B

6. ROLL NO.

0–9	0–9	0–9

7. GENDER

MALE ○

FEMALE ○

8. STREAM
(Only for Class XI and XII Students)

MATHEMATICS ○

BIOLOGY ○

OTHERS ○

9. MARK YOUR ANSWERS WITH HB PENCIL/BALL POINT PEN (BLUE/BLACK)

1.	A	B	C	D	26.	A	B	C	D
2.	A	B	C	D	27.	A	B	C	D
3.	A	B	C	D	28.	A	B	C	D
4.	A	B	C	D	29.	A	B	C	D
5.	A	B	C	D	30.	A	B	C	D
6.	A	B	C	D	31.	A	B	C	D
7.	A	B	C	D	32.	A	B	C	D
8.	A	B	C	D	33.	A	B	C	D
9.	A	B	C	D	34.	A	B	C	D
10.	A	B	C	D	35.	A	B	C	D
11.	A	B	C	D	36.	A	B	C	D
12.	A	B	C	D	37.	A	B	C	D
13.	A	B	C	D	38.	A	B	C	D
14.	A	B	C	D	39.	A	B	C	D
15.	A	B	C	D	40.	A	B	C	D
16.	A	B	C	D	41.	A	B	C	D
17.	A	B	C	D	42.	A	B	C	D
18.	A	B	C	D	43.	A	B	C	D
19.	A	B	C	D	44.	A	B	C	D
20.	A	B	C	D	45.	A	B	C	D
21.	A	B	C	D	46.	A	B	C	D
22.	A	B	C	D	47.	A	B	C	D
23.	A	B	C	D	48.	A	B	C	D
24.	A	B	C	D	49.	A	B	C	D
25.	A	B	C	D	50.	A	B	C	D

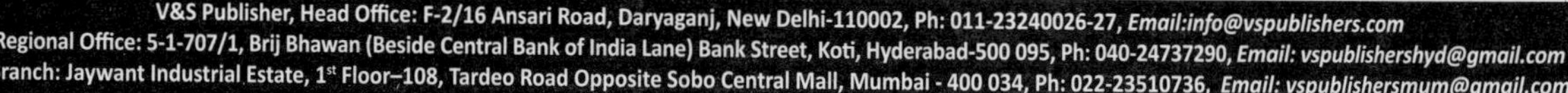
V&S Publisher, Head Office: F-2/16 Ansari Road, Daryaganj, New Delhi-110002, Ph: 011-23240026-27, *Email:info@vspublishers.com*
Regional Office: 5-1-707/1, Brij Bhawan (Beside Central Bank of India Lane) Bank Street, Koti, Hyderabad-500 095, Ph: 040-24737290, *Email: vspublishershyd@gmail.com*
Branch: Jaywant Industrial Estate, 1st Floor–108, Tardeo Road Opposite Sobo Central Mall, Mumbai - 400 034, Ph: 022-23510736, *Email: vspublishersmum@gmail.com*

OMR ANSWER SHEET

1. NAME (IN ENGLISH CAPITAL LETTERS ONLY)

2. FATHER'S NAME (IN ENGLISH CAPITAL LETTERS ONLY)

Students must write and darken the respective circles completely for School Code, Class and Roll No. columns, othewise their Answer Sheets will not be evaluated.

3. SCHOOL CODE

A–Z	A–Z	0–9	0–9	0–9	0–9

4. % of Marks | Grade

In Last Class

Percentage OR Grade

Percentage			Grade
0–9	0–9	0–9	A–J

5. CLASS

0, 1, 2	0, 1, 2, 4, 5, 6, 7, 8, 9, M, B

6. ROLL NO.

0–9	0–9	0–9

7. GENDER

MALE ○

FEMALE ○

8. STREAM
(Only for Class XI and XII Students)

MATHEMATICS ○

BIOLOGY ○

OTHERS ○

9. MARK YOUR ANSWERS WITH HB PENCIL/BALL POINT PEN (BLUE/BLACK)

No.					No.				
1.	A	B	C	D	26.	A	B	C	D
2.	A	B	C	D	27.	A	B	C	D
3.	A	B	C	D	28.	A	B	C	D
4.	A	B	C	D	29.	A	B	C	D
5.	A	B	C	D	30.	A	B	C	D
6.	A	B	C	D	31.	A	B	C	D
7.	A	B	C	D	32.	A	B	C	D
8.	A	B	C	D	33.	A	B	C	D
9.	A	B	C	D	34.	A	B	C	D
10.	A	B	C	D	35.	A	B	C	D
11.	A	B	C	D	36.	A	B	C	D
12.	A	B	C	D	37.	A	B	C	D
13.	A	B	C	D	38.	A	B	C	D
14.	A	B	C	D	39.	A	B	C	D
15.	A	B	C	D	40.	A	B	C	D
16.	A	B	C	D	41.	A	B	C	D
17.	A	B	C	D	42.	A	B	C	D
18.	A	B	C	D	43.	A	B	C	D
19.	A	B	C	D	44.	A	B	C	D
20.	A	B	C	D	45.	A	B	C	D
21.	A	B	C	D	46.	A	B	C	D
22.	A	B	C	D	47.	A	B	C	D
23.	A	B	C	D	48.	A	B	C	D
24.	A	B	C	D	49.	A	B	C	D
25.	A	B	C	D	50.	A	B	C	D

V&S Publisher, Head Office: F-2/16 Ansari Road, Daryaganj, New Delhi-110002, Ph: 011-23240026-27, *Email:info@vspublishers.com*
Regional Office: 5-1-707/1, Brij Bhawan (Beside Central Bank of India Lane) Bank Street, Koti, Hyderabad-500 095, Ph: 040-24737290, *Email: vspublishershyd@gmail.com*
Branch: Jaywant Industrial Estate, 1st Floor–108, Tardeo Road Opposite Sobo Central Mall, Mumbai - 400 034, Ph: 022-23510736, *Email: vspublishersmum@gmail.com*

OMR ANSWER SHEET

1. NAME (IN ENGLISH CAPITAL LETTERS ONLY)

2. FATHER'S NAME (IN ENGLISH CAPITAL LETTERS ONLY)

Students must write and darken the respective circles completely for School Code, Class and Roll No. columns, othewise their Answer Sheets will not be evaluated.

3. SCHOOL CODE

A	A	0	0	0	0
B	B	1	1	1	1
C	C	2	2	2	2
D	D	3	3	3	3
E	E	4	4	4	4
F	F	5	5	5	5
G	G	6	6	6	6
H	H	7	7	7	7
I	I	8	8	8	8
J	J	9	9	9	9
K	K				
L	L				
M	M				
N	N				
O	O				
P	P				
Q	Q				
R	R				
S	S				
T	T				
U	U				
V	V				
W	W				
X	X				
Y	Y				
Z	Z				

4. % of Marks / Grade

In Last Class

Percentage			OR	Grade
0	0	0		A
1	1	1		B
2	2	2		C
3	3	3		D
4	4	4		E
5	5	5		F
6	6	6		G
7	7	7		H
8	8	8		I
9	9	9		J

5. CLASS

0	0
1	1
2	2
	4
	5
	6
	7
	8
	9
	M
	B

6. ROLL NO.

0	0	0
1	1	1
2	2	2
3	3	3
4	4	4
5	5	5
6	6	6
7	7	7
8	8	8
9	9	9

7. GENDER

MALE ○

FEMALE ○

8. STREAM
(Only for Class XI and XII Students)

MATHEMATICS ○

BIOLOGY ○

OTHERS ○

9. MARK YOUR ANSWERS WITH HB PENCIL/BALL POINT PEN (BLUE/BLACK)

1.	A	B	C	D	26.	A	B	C	D
2.	A	B	C	D	27.	A	B	C	D
3.	A	B	C	D	28.	A	B	C	D
4.	A	B	C	D	29.	A	B	C	D
5.	A	B	C	D	30.	A	B	C	D
6.	A	B	C	D	31.	A	B	C	D
7.	A	B	C	D	32.	A	B	C	D
8.	A	B	C	D	33.	A	B	C	D
9.	A	B	C	D	34.	A	B	C	D
10.	A	B	C	D	35.	A	B	C	D
11.	A	B	C	D	36.	A	B	C	D
12.	A	B	C	D	37.	A	B	C	D
13.	A	B	C	D	38.	A	B	C	D
14.	A	B	C	D	39.	A	B	C	D
15.	A	B	C	D	40.	A	B	C	D
16.	A	B	C	D	41.	A	B	C	D
17.	A	B	C	D	42.	A	B	C	D
18.	A	B	C	D	43.	A	B	C	D
19.	A	B	C	D	44.	A	B	C	D
20.	A	B	C	D	45.	A	B	C	D
21.	A	B	C	D	46.	A	B	C	D
22.	A	B	C	D	47.	A	B	C	D
23.	A	B	C	D	48.	A	B	C	D
24.	A	B	C	D	49.	A	B	C	D
25.	A	B	C	D	50.	A	B	C	D

V&S Publisher, Head Office: F-2/16 Ansari Road, Daryaganj, New Delhi-110002, Ph: 011-23240026-27, *Email:info@vspublishers.com*
Regional Office: 5-1-707/1, Brij Bhawan (Beside Central Bank of India Lane) Bank Street, Koti, Hyderabad-500 095, Ph: 040-24737290, *Email: vspublishershyd@gmail.com*
Branch: Jaywant Industrial Estate, 1st Floor–108, Tardeo Road Opposite Sobo Central Mall, Mumbai - 400 034, Ph: 022-23510736, *Email: vspublishersmum@gmail.com*

OMR ANSWER SHEET

1. NAME (IN ENGLISH CAPITAL LETTERS ONLY)

2. FATHER'S NAME (IN ENGLISH CAPITAL LETTERS ONLY)

Students must write and darken the respective circles completely for School Code, Class and Roll No. columns, othewise their Answer Sheets will not be evaluated.

3. SCHOOL CODE

A–Z	A–Z	0–9	0–9	0–9	0–9

4. % of Marks / Grade

In Last Class

Percentage			OR	Grade
0–9	0–9	0–9		A–J

5. CLASS

0, 1, 2	0, 1, 2, 4, 5, 6, 7, 8, 9, M, B

6. ROLL NO.

0–9	0–9	0–9

7. GENDER

MALE ○

FEMALE ○

8. STREAM (Only for Class XI and XII Students)

MATHEMATICS ○

BIOLOGY ○

OTHERS ○

9. MARK YOUR ANSWERS WITH HB PENCIL/BALL POINT PEN (BLUE/BLACK)

Q.					Q.				
1.	A	B	C	D	26.	A	B	C	D
2.	A	B	C	D	27.	A	B	C	D
3.	A	B	C	D	28.	A	B	C	D
4.	A	B	C	D	29.	A	B	C	D
5.	A	B	C	D	30.	A	B	C	D
6.	A	B	C	D	31.	A	B	C	D
7.	A	B	C	D	32.	A	B	C	D
8.	A	B	C	D	33.	A	B	C	D
9.	A	B	C	D	34.	A	B	C	D
10.	A	B	C	D	35.	A	B	C	D
11.	A	B	C	D	36.	A	B	C	D
12.	A	B	C	D	37.	A	B	C	D
13.	A	B	C	D	38.	A	B	C	D
14.	A	B	C	D	39.	A	B	C	D
15.	A	B	C	D	40.	A	B	C	D
16.	A	B	C	D	41.	A	B	C	D
17.	A	B	C	D	42.	A	B	C	D
18.	A	B	C	D	43.	A	B	C	D
19.	A	B	C	D	44.	A	B	C	D
20.	A	B	C	D	45.	A	B	C	D
21.	A	B	C	D	46.	A	B	C	D
22.	A	B	C	D	47.	A	B	C	D
23.	A	B	C	D	48.	A	B	C	D
24.	A	B	C	D	49.	A	B	C	D
25.	A	B	C	D	50.	A	B	C	D

V&S Publisher, Head Office: F-2/16 Ansari Road, Daryaganj, New Delhi-110002, Ph: 011-23240026-27, *Email:info@vspublishers.com*
Regional Office: 5-1-707/1, Brij Bhawan (Beside Central Bank of India Lane) Bank Street, Koti, Hyderabad-500 095, Ph: 040-24737290, *Email: vspublishershyd@gmail.com*
Branch: Jaywant Industrial Estate, 1st Floor–108, Tardeo Road Opposite Sobo Central Mall, Mumbai - 400 034, Ph: 022-23510736, *Email: vspublishersmum@gmail.com*

OMR ANSWER SHEET

1. NAME (IN ENGLISH CAPITAL LETTERS ONLY)

2. FATHER'S NAME (IN ENGLISH CAPITAL LETTERS ONLY)

Students must write and darken the respective circles completely for School Code, Class and Roll No. columns, othewise their Answer Sheets will not be evaluated.

3. SCHOOL CODE

A B C D E F G H I J K L M N O P Q R S T U V W X Y Z

A B C D E F G H I J K L M N O P Q R S T U V W X Y Z

0 1 2 3 4 5 6 7 8 9 (×4)

4. % of Marks | Grade

In Last Class

Percentage OR Grade

0 1 2 3 4 5 6 7 8 9 (×3)

A B C D E F G H I J

5. CLASS

0 1 2

0 1 2 4 5 6 7 8 9 M B

6. ROLL NO.

0 1 2 3 4 5 6 7 8 9 (×3)

7. GENDER

MALE

FEMALE

8. STREAM
(Only for Class XI and XII Students)

MATHEMATICS

BIOLOGY

OTHERS

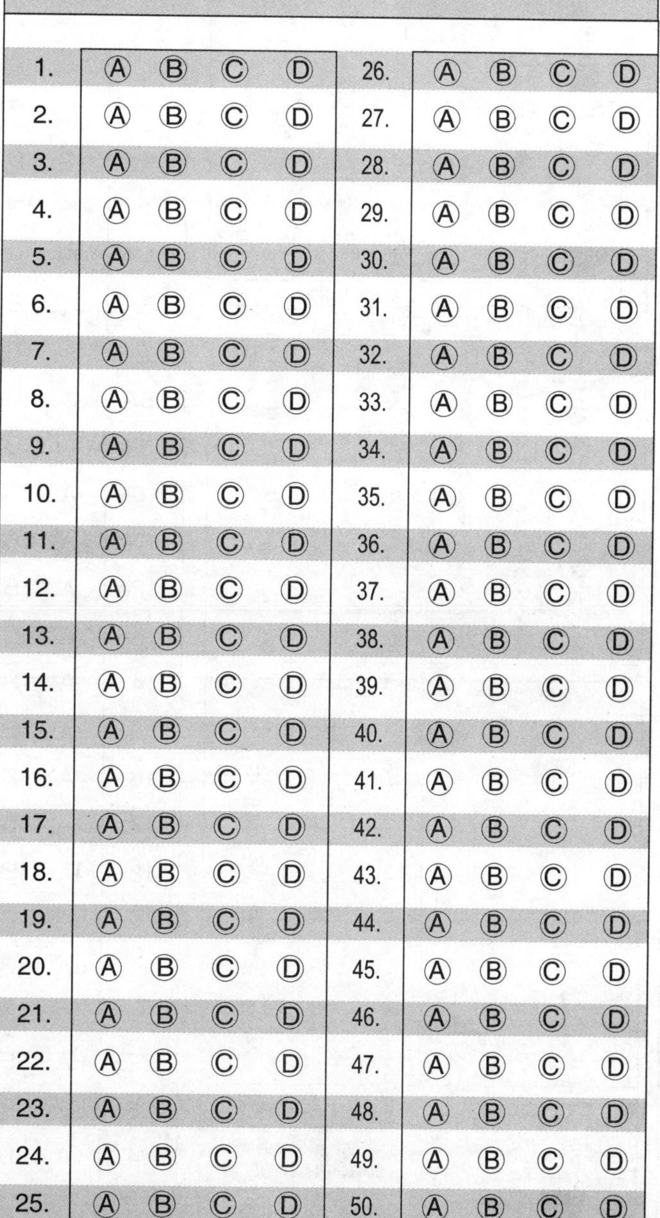

9. MARK YOUR ANSWERS WITH HB PENCIL/BALL POINT PEN (BLUE/BLACK)

1.	A	B	C	D	26.	A	B	C	D
2.	A	B	C	D	27.	A	B	C	D
3.	A	B	C	D	28.	A	B	C	D
4.	A	B	C	D	29.	A	B	C	D
5.	A	B	C	D	30.	A	B	C	D
6.	A	B	C	D	31.	A	B	C	D
7.	A	B	C	D	32.	A	B	C	D
8.	A	B	C	D	33.	A	B	C	D
9.	A	B	C	D	34.	A	B	C	D
10.	A	B	C	D	35.	A	B	C	D
11.	A	B	C	D	36.	A	B	C	D
12.	A	B	C	D	37.	A	B	C	D
13.	A	B	C	D	38.	A	B	C	D
14.	A	B	C	D	39.	A	B	C	D
15.	A	B	C	D	40.	A	B	C	D
16.	A	B	C	D	41.	A	B	C	D
17.	A	B	C	D	42.	A	B	C	D
18.	A	B	C	D	43.	A	B	C	D
19.	A	B	C	D	44.	A	B	C	D
20.	A	B	C	D	45.	A	B	C	D
21.	A	B	C	D	46.	A	B	C	D
22.	A	B	C	D	47.	A	B	C	D
23.	A	B	C	D	48.	A	B	C	D
24.	A	B	C	D	49.	A	B	C	D
25.	A	B	C	D	50.	A	B	C	D

V&S Publisher, Head Office: F-2/16 Ansari Road, Daryaganj, New Delhi-110002, Ph: 011-23240026-27, *Email:info@vspublishers.com*
Regional Office: 5-1-707/1, Brij Bhawan (Beside Central Bank of India Lane) Bank Street, Koti, Hyderabad-500 095, Ph: 040-24737290, *Email: vspublishershyd@gmail.com*
Branch: Jaywant Industrial Estate, 1st Floor–108, Tardeo Road Opposite Sobo Central Mall, Mumbai - 400 034, Ph: 022-23510736, *Email: vspublishersmum@gmail.com*

OMR ANSWER SHEET

1. NAME (IN ENGLISH CAPITAL LETTERS ONLY)

2. FATHER'S NAME (IN ENGLISH CAPITAL LETTERS ONLY)

Students must write and darken the respective circles completely for School Code, Class and Roll No. columns, othewise their Answer Sheets will not be evaluated.

3. SCHOOL CODE

A	A	0	0	0	0
B	B	1	1	1	1
C	C	2	2	2	2
D	D	3	3	3	3
E	E	4	4	4	4
F	F	5	5	5	5
G	G	6	6	6	6
H	H	7	7	7	7
I	I	8	8	8	8
J	J	9	9	9	9
K	K				
L	L				
M	M				
N	N				
O	O				
P	P				
Q	Q				
R	R				
S	S				
T	T				
U	U				
V	V				
W	W				
X	X				
Y	Y				
Z	Z				

4. % of Marks | **Grade**

In Last Class

Percentage			OR	Grade
0	0	0		A
1	1	1		B
2	2	2		C
3	3	3		D
4	4	4		E
5	5	5		F
6	6	6		G
7	7	7		H
8	8	8		I
9	9	9		J

5. CLASS

0	0
1	1
2	2
	4
	5
	6
	7
	8
	9
	M
	B

6. ROLL NO.

0	0	0
1	1	1
2	2	2
3	3	3
4	4	4
5	5	5
6	6	6
7	7	7
8	8	8
9	9	9

7. GENDER

MALE ○

FEMALE ○

8. STREAM (Only for Class XI and XII Students)

MATHEMATICS ○

BIOLOGY ○

OTHERS ○

9. MARK YOUR ANSWERS WITH HB PENCIL/BALL POINT PEN (BLUE/BLACK)

1.	A	B	C	D	26.	A	B	C	D
2.	A	B	C	D	27.	A	B	C	D
3.	A	B	C	D	28.	A	B	C	D
4.	A	B	C	D	29.	A	B	C	D
5.	A	B	C	D	30.	A	B	C	D
6.	A	B	C	D	31.	A	B	C	D
7.	A	B	C	D	32.	A	B	C	D
8.	A	B	C	D	33.	A	B	C	D
9.	A	B	C	D	34.	A	B	C	D
10.	A	B	C	D	35.	A	B	C	D
11.	A	B	C	D	36.	A	B	C	D
12.	A	B	C	D	37.	A	B	C	D
13.	A	B	C	D	38.	A	B	C	D
14.	A	B	C	D	39.	A	B	C	D
15.	A	B	C	D	40.	A	B	C	D
16.	A	B	C	D	41.	A	B	C	D
17.	A	B	C	D	42.	A	B	C	D
18.	A	B	C	D	43.	A	B	C	D
19.	A	B	C	D	44.	A	B	C	D
20.	A	B	C	D	45.	A	B	C	D
21.	A	B	C	D	46.	A	B	C	D
22.	A	B	C	D	47.	A	B	C	D
23.	A	B	C	D	48.	A	B	C	D
24.	A	B	C	D	49.	A	B	C	D
25.	A	B	C	D	50.	A	B	C	D

V&S Publisher, Head Office: F-2/16 Ansari Road, Daryaganj, New Delhi-110002, Ph: 011-23240026-27, *Email:info@vspublishers.com*
Regional Office: 5-1-707/1, Brij Bhawan (Beside Central Bank of India Lane) Bank Street, Koti, Hyderabad-500 095, Ph: 040-24737290, *Email: vspublishershyd@gmail.com*
Branch: Jaywant Industrial Estate, 1st Floor–108, Tardeo Road Opposite Sobo Central Mall, Mumbai - 400 034, Ph: 022-23510736, *Email: vspublishersmum@gmail.com*

OMR ANSWER SHEET

1. NAME (IN ENGLISH CAPITAL LETTERS ONLY)

2. FATHER'S NAME (IN ENGLISH CAPITAL LETTERS ONLY)

Students must write and darken the respective circles completely for School Code, Class and Roll No. columns, othewise their Answer Sheets will not be evaluated.

3. SCHOOL CODE

A–Z	A–Z	0–9	0–9	0–9	0–9

4. % of Marks / Grade

In Last Class

Percentage OR Grade

0–9	0–9	0–9	A–J

5. CLASS

0, 1, 2	0, 1, 2, 4, 5, 6, 7, 8, 9, M, B

6. ROLL NO.

0–9	0–9	0–9

7. GENDER

MALE ○

FEMALE ○

8. STREAM (Only for Class XI and XII Students)

MATHEMATICS ○

BIOLOGY ○

OTHERS ○

9. MARK YOUR ANSWERS WITH HB PENCIL/BALL POINT PEN (BLUE/BLACK)

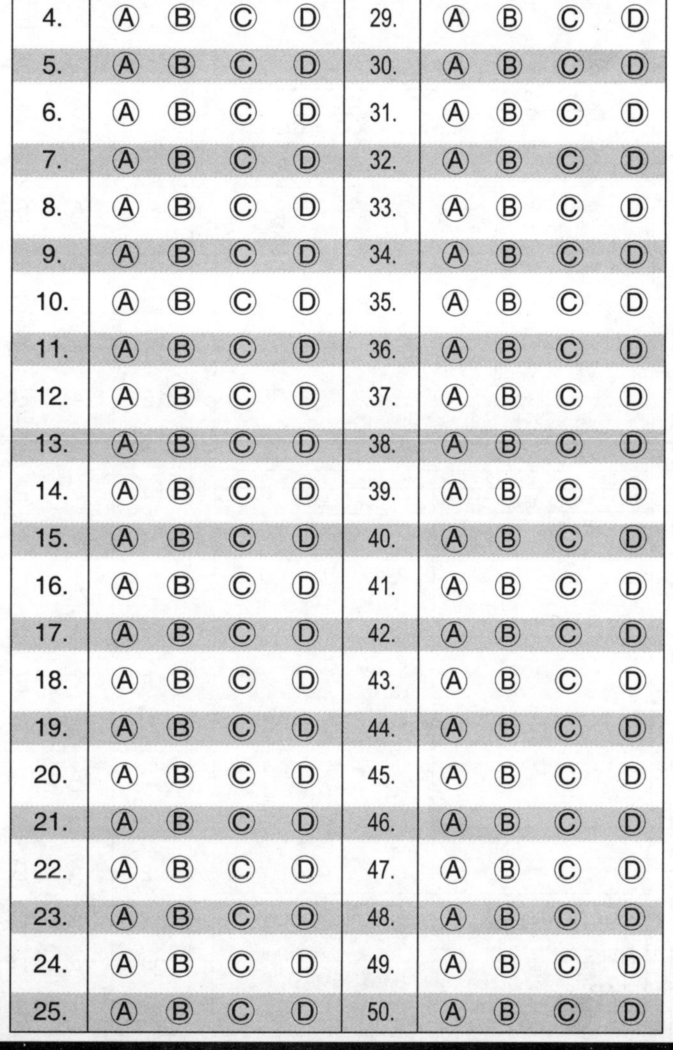

Q.					Q.				
1.	A	B	C	D	26.	A	B	C	D
2.	A	B	C	D	27.	A	B	C	D
3.	A	B	C	D	28.	A	B	C	D
4.	A	B	C	D	29.	A	B	C	D
5.	A	B	C	D	30.	A	B	C	D
6.	A	B	C	D	31.	A	B	C	D
7.	A	B	C	D	32.	A	B	C	D
8.	A	B	C	D	33.	A	B	C	D
9.	A	B	C	D	34.	A	B	C	D
10.	A	B	C	D	35.	A	B	C	D
11.	A	B	C	D	36.	A	B	C	D
12.	A	B	C	D	37.	A	B	C	D
13.	A	B	C	D	38.	A	B	C	D
14.	A	B	C	D	39.	A	B	C	D
15.	A	B	C	D	40.	A	B	C	D
16.	A	B	C	D	41.	A	B	C	D
17.	A	B	C	D	42.	A	B	C	D
18.	A	B	C	D	43.	A	B	C	D
19.	A	B	C	D	44.	A	B	C	D
20.	A	B	C	D	45.	A	B	C	D
21.	A	B	C	D	46.	A	B	C	D
22.	A	B	C	D	47.	A	B	C	D
23.	A	B	C	D	48.	A	B	C	D
24.	A	B	C	D	49.	A	B	C	D
25.	A	B	C	D	50.	A	B	C	D

V&S Publisher, Head Office: F-2/16 Ansari Road, Daryaganj, New Delhi-110002, Ph: 011-23240026-27, *Email:info@vspublishers.com*

Regional Office: 5-1-707/1, Brij Bhawan (Beside Central Bank of India Lane) Bank Street, Koti, Hyderabad-500 095, Ph: 040-24737290, *Email: vspublishershyd@gmail.com*

Branch: Jaywant Industrial Estate, 1st Floor–108, Tardeo Road Opposite Sobo Central Mall, Mumbai - 400 034, Ph: 022-23510736, *Email: vspublishersmum@gmail.com*

OMR ANSWER SHEET

1. NAME (IN ENGLISH CAPITAL LETTERS ONLY)

2. FATHER'S NAME (IN ENGLISH CAPITAL LETTERS ONLY)

Students must write and darken the respective circles completely for School Code, Class and Roll No. columns, othewise their Answer Sheets will not be evaluated.

3. SCHOOL CODE

A	A	0	0	0	0
B	B	1	1	1	1
C	C	2	2	2	2
D	D	3	3	3	3
E	E	4	4	4	4
F	F	5	5	5	5
G	G	6	6	6	6
H	H	7	7	7	7
I	I	8	8	8	8
J	J	9	9	9	9
K	K				
L	L				
M	M				
N	N				
O	O				
P	P				
Q	Q				
R	R				
S	S				
T	T				
U	U				
V	V				
W	W				
X	X				
Y	Y				
Z	Z				

4. % of Marks | Grade

In Last Class

Percentage			OR	Grade
0	0	0		A
1	1	1		B
2	2	2		C
3	3	3		D
4	4	4		E
5	5	5		F
6	6	6		G
7	7	7		H
8	8	8		I
9	9	9		J

5. CLASS		6. ROLL NO.		
0	0	0	0	0
1	1	1	1	1
2	2	2	2	2
	4	3	3	3
	5	4	4	4
	6	5	5	5
	7	6	6	6
	8	7	7	7
	9	8	8	8
	M	9	9	9
	B			

7. GENDER

MALE ○

FEMALE ○

8. STREAM
(Only for Class XI and XII Students)

MATHEMATICS ○

BIOLOGY ○

OTHERS ○

9. MARK YOUR ANSWERS WITH HB PENCIL/BALL POINT PEN (BLUE/BLACK)

Q.					Q.				
1.	A	B	C	D	26.	A	B	C	D
2.	A	B	C	D	27.	A	B	C	D
3.	A	B	C	D	28.	A	B	C	D
4.	A	B	C	D	29.	A	B	C	D
5.	A	B	C	D	30.	A	B	C	D
6.	A	B	C	D	31.	A	B	C	D
7.	A	B	C	D	32.	A	B	C	D
8.	A	B	C	D	33.	A	B	C	D
9.	A	B	C	D	34.	A	B	C	D
10.	A	B	C	D	35.	A	B	C	D
11.	A	B	C	D	36.	A	B	C	D
12.	A	B	C	D	37.	A	B	C	D
13.	A	B	C	D	38.	A	B	C	D
14.	A	B	C	D	39.	A	B	C	D
15.	A	B	C	D	40.	A	B	C	D
16.	A	B	C	D	41.	A	B	C	D
17.	A	B	C	D	42.	A	B	C	D
18.	A	B	C	D	43.	A	B	C	D
19.	A	B	C	D	44.	A	B	C	D
20.	A	B	C	D	45.	A	B	C	D
21.	A	B	C	D	46.	A	B	C	D
22.	A	B	C	D	47.	A	B	C	D
23.	A	B	C	D	48.	A	B	C	D
24.	A	B	C	D	49.	A	B	C	D
25.	A	B	C	D	50.	A	B	C	D

V&S Publisher, Head Office: F-2/16 Ansari Road, Daryaganj, New Delhi-110002, Ph: 011-23240026-27, *Email:info@vspublishers.com*

Regional Office: 5-1-707/1, Brij Bhawan (Beside Central Bank of India Lane) Bank Street, Koti, Hyderabad-500 095, Ph: 040-24737290, *Email: vspublishershyd@gmail.com*

Branch: Jaywant Industrial Estate, 1st Floor–108, Tardeo Road Opposite Sobo Central Mall, Mumbai - 400 034, Ph: 022-23510736, *Email: vspublishersmum@gmail.com*

OMR ANSWER SHEET

1. NAME (IN ENGLISH CAPITAL LETTERS ONLY)

2. FATHER'S NAME (IN ENGLISH CAPITAL LETTERS ONLY)

Students must write and darken the respective circles completely for School Code, Class and Roll No. columns, othewise their Answer Sheets will not be evaluated.

3. SCHOOL CODE

A–Z	A–Z	0–9	0–9	0–9	0–9

4. % of Marks / Grade

In Last Class

Percentage OR Grade

Percentage			Grade
0–9	0–9	0–9	A–J

5. CLASS

0, 1, 2	0, 1, 2, 4, 5, 6, 7, 8, 9, M, B

6. ROLL NO.

0–9	0–9	0–9

7. GENDER

MALE ○

FEMALE ○

8. STREAM (Only for Class XI and XII Students)

MATHEMATICS ○

BIOLOGY ○

OTHERS ○

9. MARK YOUR ANSWERS WITH HB PENCIL/BALL POINT PEN (BLUE/BLACK)

No.					No.				
1.	A	B	C	D	26.	A	B	C	D
2.	A	B	C	D	27.	A	B	C	D
3.	A	B	C	D	28.	A	B	C	D
4.	A	B	C	D	29.	A	B	C	D
5.	A	B	C	D	30.	A	B	C	D
6.	A	B	C	D	31.	A	B	C	D
7.	A	B	C	D	32.	A	B	C	D
8.	A	B	C	D	33.	A	B	C	D
9.	A	B	C	D	34.	A	B	C	D
10.	A	B	C	D	35.	A	B	C	D
11.	A	B	C	D	36.	A	B	C	D
12.	A	B	C	D	37.	A	B	C	D
13.	A	B	C	D	38.	A	B	C	D
14.	A	B	C	D	39.	A	B	C	D
15.	A	B	C	D	40.	A	B	C	D
16.	A	B	C	D	41.	A	B	C	D
17.	A	B	C	D	42.	A	B	C	D
18.	A	B	C	D	43.	A	B	C	D
19.	A	B	C	D	44.	A	B	C	D
20.	A	B	C	D	45.	A	B	C	D
21.	A	B	C	D	46.	A	B	C	D
22.	A	B	C	D	47.	A	B	C	D
23.	A	B	C	D	48.	A	B	C	D
24.	A	B	C	D	49.	A	B	C	D
25.	A	B	C	D	50.	A	B	C	D

V&S Publisher, Head Office: F-2/16 Ansari Road, Daryaganj, New Delhi-110002, Ph: 011-23240026-27, *Email:info@vspublishers.com*
Regional Office: 5-1-707/1, Brij Bhawan (Beside Central Bank of India Lane) Bank Street, Koti, Hyderabad-500 095, Ph: 040-24737290, *Email: vspublishershyd@gmail.com*
Branch: Jaywant Industrial Estate, 1st Floor–108, Tardeo Road Opposite Sobo Central Mall, Mumbai - 400 034, Ph: 022-23510736, *Email: vspublishersmum@gmail.com*

OMR ANSWER SHEET

1. NAME (IN ENGLISH CAPITAL LETTERS ONLY)

2. FATHER'S NAME (IN ENGLISH CAPITAL LETTERS ONLY)

Students must write and darken the respective circles completely for School Code, Class and Roll No. columns, othewise their Answer Sheets will not be evaluated.

3. SCHOOL CODE

A–Z	A–Z	0–9	0–9	0–9	0–9

4. % of Marks / Grade

In Last Class

Percentage OR Grade

0–9	0–9	0–9	A–J

5. CLASS

0, 1, 2	0, 1, 2, 4, 5, 6, 7, 8, 9, M, B

6. ROLL NO.

0–9	0–9	0–9

7. GENDER

MALE ○

FEMALE ○

8. STREAM
(Only for Class XI and XII Students)

MATHEMATICS ○

BIOLOGY ○

OTHERS ○

9. MARK YOUR ANSWERS WITH HB PENCIL/BALL POINT PEN (BLUE/BLACK)

1.	A	B	C	D	26.	A	B	C	D
2.	A	B	C	D	27.	A	B	C	D
3.	A	B	C	D	28.	A	B	C	D
4.	A	B	C	D	29.	A	B	C	D
5.	A	B	C	D	30.	A	B	C	D
6.	A	B	C	D	31.	A	B	C	D
7.	A	B	C	D	32.	A	B	C	D
8.	A	B	C	D	33.	A	B	C	D
9.	A	B	C	D	34.	A	B	C	D
10.	A	B	C	D	35.	A	B	C	D
11.	A	B	C	D	36.	A	B	C	D
12.	A	B	C	D	37.	A	B	C	D
13.	A	B	C	D	38.	A	B	C	D
14.	A	B	C	D	39.	A	B	C	D
15.	A	B	C	D	40.	A	B	C	D
16.	A	B	C	D	41.	A	B	C	D
17.	A	B	C	D	42.	A	B	C	D
18.	A	B	C	D	43.	A	B	C	D
19.	A	B	C	D	44.	A	B	C	D
20.	A	B	C	D	45.	A	B	C	D
21.	A	B	C	D	46.	A	B	C	D
22.	A	B	C	D	47.	A	B	C	D
23.	A	B	C	D	48.	A	B	C	D
24.	A	B	C	D	49.	A	B	C	D
25.	A	B	C	D	50.	A	B	C	D

V&S Publisher, Head Office: F-2/16 Ansari Road, Daryaganj, New Delhi-110002, Ph: 011-23240026-27, *Email:info@vspublishers.com*
Regional Office: 5-1-707/1, Brij Bhawan (Beside Central Bank of India Lane) Bank Street, Koti, Hyderabad-500 095, Ph: 040-24737290, *Email: vspublishershyd@gmail.com*
Branch: Jaywant Industrial Estate, 1st Floor–108, Tardeo Road Opposite Sobo Central Mall, Mumbai - 400 034, Ph: 022-23510736, *Email: vspublishersmum@gmail.com*

OMR ANSWER SHEET

1. NAME (IN ENGLISH CAPITAL LETTERS ONLY)

2. FATHER'S NAME (IN ENGLISH CAPITAL LETTERS ONLY)

Students must write and darken the respective circles completely for School Code, Class and Roll No. columns, othewise their Answer Sheets will not be evaluated.

3. SCHOOL CODE

A–Z	A–Z	0–9	0–9	0–9	0–9

4. % of Marks | Grade

In Last Class

Percentage OR Grade

0–9	0–9	0–9	A–J

5. CLASS

0, 1, 2	0, 1, 2, 4, 5, 6, 7, 8, 9, M, B

6. ROLL NO.

0–9	0–9	0–9

7. GENDER

MALE ○

FEMALE ○

8. STREAM
(Only for Class XI and XII Students)

MATHEMATICS ○

BIOLOGY ○

OTHERS ○

9. MARK YOUR ANSWERS WITH HB PENCIL/BALL POINT PEN (BLUE/BLACK)

No.					No.				
1.	A	B	C	D	26.	A	B	C	D
2.	A	B	C	D	27.	A	B	C	D
3.	A	B	C	D	28.	A	B	C	D
4.	A	B	C	D	29.	A	B	C	D
5.	A	B	C	D	30.	A	B	C	D
6.	A	B	C	D	31.	A	B	C	D
7.	A	B	C	D	32.	A	B	C	D
8.	A	B	C	D	33.	A	B	C	D
9.	A	B	C	D	34.	A	B	C	D
10.	A	B	C	D	35.	A	B	C	D
11.	A	B	C	D	36.	A	B	C	D
12.	A	B	C	D	37.	A	B	C	D
13.	A	B	C	D	38.	A	B	C	D
14.	A	B	C	D	39.	A	B	C	D
15.	A	B	C	D	40.	A	B	C	D
16.	A	B	C	D	41.	A	B	C	D
17.	A	B	C	D	42.	A	B	C	D
18.	A	B	C	D	43.	A	B	C	D
19.	A	B	C	D	44.	A	B	C	D
20.	A	B	C	D	45.	A	B	C	D
21.	A	B	C	D	46.	A	B	C	D
22.	A	B	C	D	47.	A	B	C	D
23.	A	B	C	D	48.	A	B	C	D
24.	A	B	C	D	49.	A	B	C	D
25.	A	B	C	D	50.	A	B	C	D

V&S Publisher, Head Office: F-2/16 Ansari Road, Daryaganj, New Delhi-110002, Ph: 011-23240026-27, Email:info@vspublishers.com
Regional Office: 5-1-707/1, Brij Bhawan (Beside Central Bank of India Lane) Bank Street, Koti, Hyderabad-500 095, Ph: 040-24737290, Email: vspublishershyd@gmail.com
Branch: Jaywant Industrial Estate, 1st Floor–108, Tardeo Road Opposite Sobo Central Mall, Mumbai - 400 034, Ph: 022-23510736, Email: vspublishersmum@gmail.com

OMR ANSWER SHEET

1. NAME (IN ENGLISH CAPITAL LETTERS ONLY)

2. FATHER'S NAME (IN ENGLISH CAPITAL LETTERS ONLY)

Students must write and darken the respective circles completely for School Code, Class and Roll No. columns, othewise their Answer Sheets will not be evaluated.

3. SCHOOL CODE

A	A	0	0	0	0
B	B	1	1	1	1
C	C	2	2	2	2
D	D	3	3	3	3
E	E	4	4	4	4
F	F	5	5	5	5
G	G	6	6	6	6
H	H	7	7	7	7
I	I	8	8	8	8
J	J	9	9	9	9
K	K				
L	L				
M	M				
N	N				
O	O				
P	P				
Q	Q				
R	R				
S	S				
T	T				
U	U				
V	V				
W	W				
X	X				
Y	Y				
Z	Z				

4. % of Marks | Grade

In Last Class

Percentage			OR	Grade
0	0	0		A
1	1	1		B
2	2	2		C
3	3	3		D
4	4	4		E
5	5	5		F
6	6	6		G
7	7	7		H
8	8	8		I
9	9	9		J

5. CLASS		6. ROLL NO.		
0	0	0	0	0
1	1	1	1	1
2	2	2	2	2
	4	3	3	3
	5	4	4	4
	6	5	5	5
	7	6	6	6
	8	7	7	7
	9	8	8	8
	M	9	9	9
	B			

7. GENDER

MALE ○
FEMALE ○

8. STREAM
(Only for Class XI and XII Students)

MATHEMATICS ○
BIOLOGY ○
OTHERS ○

9. MARK YOUR ANSWERS WITH HB PENCIL/BALL POINT PEN (BLUE/BLACK)

1.	A	B	C	D	26.	A	B	C	D
2.	A	B	C	D	27.	A	B	C	D
3.	A	B	C	D	28.	A	B	C	D
4.	A	B	C	D	29.	A	B	C	D
5.	A	B	C	D	30.	A	B	C	D
6.	A	B	C	D	31.	A	B	C	D
7.	A	B	C	D	32.	A	B	C	D
8.	A	B	C	D	33.	A	B	C	D
9.	A	B	C	D	34.	A	B	C	D
10.	A	B	C	D	35.	A	B	C	D
11.	A	B	C	D	36.	A	B	C	D
12.	A	B	C	D	37.	A	B	C	D
13.	A	B	C	D	38.	A	B	C	D
14.	A	B	C	D	39.	A	B	C	D
15.	A	B	C	D	40.	A	B	C	D
16.	A	B	C	D	41.	A	B	C	D
17.	A	B	C	D	42.	A	B	C	D
18.	A	B	C	D	43.	A	B	C	D
19.	A	B	C	D	44.	A	B	C	D
20.	A	B	C	D	45.	A	B	C	D
21.	A	B	C	D	46.	A	B	C	D
22.	A	B	C	D	47.	A	B	C	D
23.	A	B	C	D	48.	A	B	C	D
24.	A	B	C	D	49.	A	B	C	D
25.	A	B	C	D	50.	A	B	C	D

V&S Publisher, Head Office: F-2/16 Ansari Road, Daryaganj, New Delhi-110002, Ph: 011-23240026-27, *Email:info@vspublishers.com*
Regional Office: 5-1-707/1, Brij Bhawan (Beside Central Bank of India Lane) Bank Street, Koti, Hyderabad-500 095, Ph: 040-24737290, *Email: vspublishershyd@gmail.com*
Branch: Jaywant Industrial Estate, 1st Floor–108, Tardeo Road Opposite Sobo Central Mall, Mumbai - 400 034, Ph: 022-23510736, *Email: vspublishersmum@gmail.com*

OMR ANSWER SHEET

1. NAME (IN ENGLISH CAPITAL LETTERS ONLY)

2. FATHER'S NAME (IN ENGLISH CAPITAL LETTERS ONLY)

Students must write and darken the respective circles completely for School Code, Class and Roll No. columns, othewise their Answer Sheets will not be evaluated.

3. SCHOOL CODE

A–Z	A–Z	0–9	0–9	0–9	0–9

4. % of Marks | Grade

In Last Class

Percentage OR Grade

0–9	0–9	0–9	A–J

5. CLASS

0, 1, 2	0, 1, 2, 4, 5, 6, 7, 8, 9, M, B

6. ROLL NO.

0–9	0–9	0–9

7. GENDER

MALE ○

FEMALE ○

8. STREAM
(Only for Class XI and XII Students)

MATHEMATICS ○

BIOLOGY ○

OTHERS ○

9. MARK YOUR ANSWERS WITH HB PENCIL/BALL POINT PEN (BLUE/BLACK)

1.	Ⓐ	Ⓑ	Ⓒ	Ⓓ	26.	Ⓐ	Ⓑ	Ⓒ	Ⓓ
2.	Ⓐ	Ⓑ	Ⓒ	Ⓓ	27.	Ⓐ	Ⓑ	Ⓒ	Ⓓ
3.	Ⓐ	Ⓑ	Ⓒ	Ⓓ	28.	Ⓐ	Ⓑ	Ⓒ	Ⓓ
4.	Ⓐ	Ⓑ	Ⓒ	Ⓓ	29.	Ⓐ	Ⓑ	Ⓒ	Ⓓ
5.	Ⓐ	Ⓑ	Ⓒ	Ⓓ	30.	Ⓐ	Ⓑ	Ⓒ	Ⓓ
6.	Ⓐ	Ⓑ	Ⓒ	Ⓓ	31.	Ⓐ	Ⓑ	Ⓒ	Ⓓ
7.	Ⓐ	Ⓑ	Ⓒ	Ⓓ	32.	Ⓐ	Ⓑ	Ⓒ	Ⓓ
8.	Ⓐ	Ⓑ	Ⓒ	Ⓓ	33.	Ⓐ	Ⓑ	Ⓒ	Ⓓ
9.	Ⓐ	Ⓑ	Ⓒ	Ⓓ	34.	Ⓐ	Ⓑ	Ⓒ	Ⓓ
10.	Ⓐ	Ⓑ	Ⓒ	Ⓓ	35.	Ⓐ	Ⓑ	Ⓒ	Ⓓ
11.	Ⓐ	Ⓑ	Ⓒ	Ⓓ	36.	Ⓐ	Ⓑ	Ⓒ	Ⓓ
12.	Ⓐ	Ⓑ	Ⓒ	Ⓓ	37.	Ⓐ	Ⓑ	Ⓒ	Ⓓ
13.	Ⓐ	Ⓑ	Ⓒ	Ⓓ	38.	Ⓐ	Ⓑ	Ⓒ	Ⓓ
14.	Ⓐ	Ⓑ	Ⓒ	Ⓓ	39.	Ⓐ	Ⓑ	Ⓒ	Ⓓ
15.	Ⓐ	Ⓑ	Ⓒ	Ⓓ	40.	Ⓐ	Ⓑ	Ⓒ	Ⓓ
16.	Ⓐ	Ⓑ	Ⓒ	Ⓓ	41.	Ⓐ	Ⓑ	Ⓒ	Ⓓ
17.	Ⓐ	Ⓑ	Ⓒ	Ⓓ	42.	Ⓐ	Ⓑ	Ⓒ	Ⓓ
18.	Ⓐ	Ⓑ	Ⓒ	Ⓓ	43.	Ⓐ	Ⓑ	Ⓒ	Ⓓ
19.	Ⓐ	Ⓑ	Ⓒ	Ⓓ	44.	Ⓐ	Ⓑ	Ⓒ	Ⓓ
20.	Ⓐ	Ⓑ	Ⓒ	Ⓓ	45.	Ⓐ	Ⓑ	Ⓒ	Ⓓ
21.	Ⓐ	Ⓑ	Ⓒ	Ⓓ	46.	Ⓐ	Ⓑ	Ⓒ	Ⓓ
22.	Ⓐ	Ⓑ	Ⓒ	Ⓓ	47.	Ⓐ	Ⓑ	Ⓒ	Ⓓ
23.	Ⓐ	Ⓑ	Ⓒ	Ⓓ	48.	Ⓐ	Ⓑ	Ⓒ	Ⓓ
24.	Ⓐ	Ⓑ	Ⓒ	Ⓓ	49.	Ⓐ	Ⓑ	Ⓒ	Ⓓ
25.	Ⓐ	Ⓑ	Ⓒ	Ⓓ	50.	Ⓐ	Ⓑ	Ⓒ	Ⓓ

V&S Publisher, Head Office: F-2/16 Ansari Road, Daryaganj, New Delhi-110002, Ph: 011-23240026-27, *Email:info@vspublishers.com*
Regional Office: 5-1-707/1, Brij Bhawan (Beside Central Bank of India Lane) Bank Street, Koti, Hyderabad-500 095, Ph: 040-24737290, *Email: vspublishershyd@gmail.com*
Branch: Jaywant Industrial Estate, 1st Floor–108, Tardeo Road Opposite Sobo Central Mall, Mumbai - 400 034, Ph: 022-23510736, *Email: vspublishersmum@gmail.com*

OMR ANSWER SHEET

1. NAME (IN ENGLISH CAPITAL LETTERS ONLY)

2. FATHER'S NAME (IN ENGLISH CAPITAL LETTERS ONLY)

Students must write and darken the respective circles completely for School Code, Class and Roll No. columns, othewise their Answer Sheets will not be evaluated.

3. SCHOOL CODE

A B C D E F G H I J K L M N O P Q R S T U V W X Y Z

A B C D E F G H I J K L M N O P Q R S T U V W X Y Z

0 1 2 3 4 5 6 7 8 9

0 1 2 3 4 5 6 7 8 9

0 1 2 3 4 5 6 7 8 9

0 1 2 3 4 5 6 7 8 9

4. % of Marks | Grade

In Last Class

Percentage OR Grade

Percentage			Grade
0	0	0	A
1	1	1	B
2	2	2	C
3	3	3	D
4	4	4	E
5	5	5	F
6	6	6	G
7	7	7	H
8	8	8	I
9	9	9	J

5. CLASS

0 1 2

0 1 2 4 5 6 7 8 9 M B

6. ROLL NO.

0 1 2 3 4 5 6 7 8 9

0 1 2 3 4 5 6 7 8 9

0 1 2 3 4 5 6 7 8 9

7. GENDER

MALE ○

FEMALE ○

8. STREAM
(Only for Class XI and XII Students)

MATHEMATICS ○

BIOLOGY ○

OTHERS ○

9. MARK YOUR ANSWERS WITH HB PENCIL/BALL POINT PEN (BLUE/BLACK)

1.	A	B	C	D	26.	A	B	C	D
2.	A	B	C	D	27.	A	B	C	D
3.	A	B	C	D	28.	A	B	C	D
4.	A	B	C	D	29.	A	B	C	D
5.	A	B	C	D	30.	A	B	C	D
6.	A	B	C	D	31.	A	B	C	D
7.	A	B	C	D	32.	A	B	C	D
8.	A	B	C	D	33.	A	B	C	D
9.	A	B	C	D	34.	A	B	C	D
10.	A	B	C	D	35.	A	B	C	D
11.	A	B	C	D	36.	A	B	C	D
12.	A	B	C	D	37.	A	B	C	D
13.	A	B	C	D	38.	A	B	C	D
14.	A	B	C	D	39.	A	B	C	D
15.	A	B	C	D	40.	A	B	C	D
16.	A	B	C	D	41.	A	B	C	D
17.	A	B	C	D	42.	A	B	C	D
18.	A	B	C	D	43.	A	B	C	D
19.	A	B	C	D	44.	A	B	C	D
20.	A	B	C	D	45.	A	B	C	D
21.	A	B	C	D	46.	A	B	C	D
22.	A	B	C	D	47.	A	B	C	D
23.	A	B	C	D	48.	A	B	C	D
24.	A	B	C	D	49.	A	B	C	D
25.	A	B	C	D	50.	A	B	C	D

V&S Publisher, Head Office: F-2/16 Ansari Road, Daryaganj, New Delhi-110002, Ph: 011-23240026-27, *Email:info@vspublishers.com*
Regional Office: 5-1-707/1, Brij Bhawan (Beside Central Bank of India Lane) Bank Street, Koti, Hyderabad-500 095, Ph: 040-24737290, *Email: vspublishershyd@gmail.com*
Branch: Jaywant Industrial Estate, 1st Floor–108, Tardeo Road Opposite Sobo Central Mall, Mumbai - 400 034, Ph: 022-23510736, *Email: vspublishersmum@gmail.com*

OMR ANSWER SHEET

1. NAME (IN ENGLISH CAPITAL LETTERS ONLY)

2. FATHER'S NAME (IN ENGLISH CAPITAL LETTERS ONLY)

Students must write and darken the respective circles completely for School Code, Class and Roll No. columns, othewise their Answer Sheets will not be evaluated.

3. SCHOOL CODE

A–Z	A–Z	0–9	0–9	0–9	0–9

4. % of Marks / Grade

In Last Class

Percentage OR Grade

0–9	0–9	0–9	A–J

5. CLASS

0, 1, 2	0, 1, 2, 4, 5, 6, 7, 8, 9, M, B

6. ROLL NO.

0–9	0–9	0–9

7. GENDER

MALE ○

FEMALE ○

8. STREAM

(Only for Class XI and XII Students)

MATHEMATICS ○

BIOLOGY ○

OTHERS ○

9. MARK YOUR ANSWERS WITH HB PENCIL/BALL POINT PEN (BLUE/BLACK)

1.	Ⓐ	Ⓑ	Ⓒ	Ⓓ	26.	Ⓐ	Ⓑ	Ⓒ	Ⓓ
2.	Ⓐ	Ⓑ	Ⓒ	Ⓓ	27.	Ⓐ	Ⓑ	Ⓒ	Ⓓ
3.	Ⓐ	Ⓑ	Ⓒ	Ⓓ	28.	Ⓐ	Ⓑ	Ⓒ	Ⓓ
4.	Ⓐ	Ⓑ	Ⓒ	Ⓓ	29.	Ⓐ	Ⓑ	Ⓒ	Ⓓ
5.	Ⓐ	Ⓑ	Ⓒ	Ⓓ	30.	Ⓐ	Ⓑ	Ⓒ	Ⓓ
6.	Ⓐ	Ⓑ	Ⓒ	Ⓓ	31.	Ⓐ	Ⓑ	Ⓒ	Ⓓ
7.	Ⓐ	Ⓑ	Ⓒ	Ⓓ	32.	Ⓐ	Ⓑ	Ⓒ	Ⓓ
8.	Ⓐ	Ⓑ	Ⓒ	Ⓓ	33.	Ⓐ	Ⓑ	Ⓒ	Ⓓ
9.	Ⓐ	Ⓑ	Ⓒ	Ⓓ	34.	Ⓐ	Ⓑ	Ⓒ	Ⓓ
10.	Ⓐ	Ⓑ	Ⓒ	Ⓓ	35.	Ⓐ	Ⓑ	Ⓒ	Ⓓ
11.	Ⓐ	Ⓑ	Ⓒ	Ⓓ	36.	Ⓐ	Ⓑ	Ⓒ	Ⓓ
12.	Ⓐ	Ⓑ	Ⓒ	Ⓓ	37.	Ⓐ	Ⓑ	Ⓒ	Ⓓ
13.	Ⓐ	Ⓑ	Ⓒ	Ⓓ	38.	Ⓐ	Ⓑ	Ⓒ	Ⓓ
14.	Ⓐ	Ⓑ	Ⓒ	Ⓓ	39.	Ⓐ	Ⓑ	Ⓒ	Ⓓ
15.	Ⓐ	Ⓑ	Ⓒ	Ⓓ	40.	Ⓐ	Ⓑ	Ⓒ	Ⓓ
16.	Ⓐ	Ⓑ	Ⓒ	Ⓓ	41.	Ⓐ	Ⓑ	Ⓒ	Ⓓ
17.	Ⓐ	Ⓑ	Ⓒ	Ⓓ	42.	Ⓐ	Ⓑ	Ⓒ	Ⓓ
18.	Ⓐ	Ⓑ	Ⓒ	Ⓓ	43.	Ⓐ	Ⓑ	Ⓒ	Ⓓ
19.	Ⓐ	Ⓑ	Ⓒ	Ⓓ	44.	Ⓐ	Ⓑ	Ⓒ	Ⓓ
20.	Ⓐ	Ⓑ	Ⓒ	Ⓓ	45.	Ⓐ	Ⓑ	Ⓒ	Ⓓ
21.	Ⓐ	Ⓑ	Ⓒ	Ⓓ	46.	Ⓐ	Ⓑ	Ⓒ	Ⓓ
22.	Ⓐ	Ⓑ	Ⓒ	Ⓓ	47.	Ⓐ	Ⓑ	Ⓒ	Ⓓ
23.	Ⓐ	Ⓑ	Ⓒ	Ⓓ	48.	Ⓐ	Ⓑ	Ⓒ	Ⓓ
24.	Ⓐ	Ⓑ	Ⓒ	Ⓓ	49.	Ⓐ	Ⓑ	Ⓒ	Ⓓ
25.	Ⓐ	Ⓑ	Ⓒ	Ⓓ	50.	Ⓐ	Ⓑ	Ⓒ	Ⓓ

V&S Publisher, Head Office: F-2/16 Ansari Road, Daryaganj, New Delhi-110002, Ph: 011-23240026-27, *Email:info@vspublishers.com*
Regional Office: 5-1-707/1, Brij Bhawan (Beside Central Bank of India Lane) Bank Street, Koti, Hyderabad-500 095, Ph: 040-24737290, *Email: vspublishershyd@gmail.com*
Branch: Jaywant Industrial Estate, 1st Floor–108, Tardeo Road Opposite Sobo Central Mall, Mumbai - 400 034, Ph: 022-23510736, *Email: vspublishersmum@gmail.com*

OMR ANSWER SHEET

1. NAME (IN ENGLISH CAPITAL LETTERS ONLY)

2. FATHER'S NAME (IN ENGLISH CAPITAL LETTERS ONLY)

Students must write and darken the respective circles completely for School Code, Class and Roll No. columns, othewise their Answer Sheets will not be evaluated.

3. SCHOOL CODE

A–Z	A–Z	0–9	0–9	0–9	0–9

4. % of Marks | Grade

In Last Class

Percentage			OR	Grade
0–9	0–9	0–9		A–J

5. CLASS

0, 1, 2	0, 1, 2, 4, 5, 6, 7, 8, 9, M, B

6. ROLL NO.

0–9	0–9	0–9

7. GENDER

MALE ○

FEMALE ○

8. STREAM (Only for Class XI and XII Students)

MATHEMATICS ○

BIOLOGY ○

OTHERS ○

9. MARK YOUR ANSWERS WITH HB PENCIL/BALL POINT PEN (BLUE/BLACK)

No.					No.				
1.	A	B	C	D	26.	A	B	C	D
2.	A	B	C	D	27.	A	B	C	D
3.	A	B	C	D	28.	A	B	C	D
4.	A	B	C	D	29.	A	B	C	D
5.	A	B	C	D	30.	A	B	C	D
6.	A	B	C	D	31.	A	B	C	D
7.	A	B	C	D	32.	A	B	C	D
8.	A	B	C	D	33.	A	B	C	D
9.	A	B	C	D	34.	A	B	C	D
10.	A	B	C	D	35.	A	B	C	D
11.	A	B	C	D	36.	A	B	C	D
12.	A	B	C	D	37.	A	B	C	D
13.	A	B	C	D	38.	A	B	C	D
14.	A	B	C	D	39.	A	B	C	D
15.	A	B	C	D	40.	A	B	C	D
16.	A	B	C	D	41.	A	B	C	D
17.	A	B	C	D	42.	A	B	C	D
18.	A	B	C	D	43.	A	B	C	D
19.	A	B	C	D	44.	A	B	C	D
20.	A	B	C	D	45.	A	B	C	D
21.	A	B	C	D	46.	A	B	C	D
22.	A	B	C	D	47.	A	B	C	D
23.	A	B	C	D	48.	A	B	C	D
24.	A	B	C	D	49.	A	B	C	D
25.	A	B	C	D	50.	A	B	C	D

V&S Publisher, Head Office: F-2/16 Ansari Road, Daryaganj, New Delhi-110002, Ph: 011-23240026-27, *Email:info@vspublishers.com*

Regional Office: 5-1-707/1, Brij Bhawan (Beside Central Bank of India Lane) Bank Street, Koti, Hyderabad-500 095, Ph: 040-24737290, *Email: vspublishershyd@gmail.com*

Branch: Jaywant Industrial Estate, 1st Floor–108, Tardeo Road Opposite Sobo Central Mall, Mumbai - 400 034, Ph: 022-23510736, *Email: vspublishersmum@gmail.com*